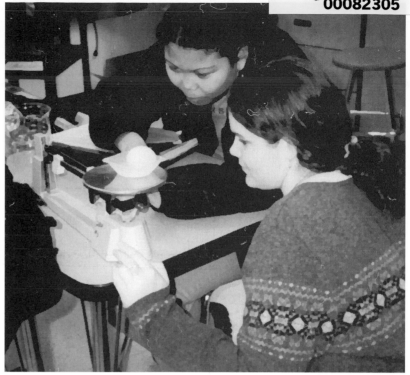

HUMAN
BODY
EXPLORATIONS

Hands-On Investigations
of What Makes Us Tick

D0557103

Karen E. Kalumuck, Ph.D.
and the Exploratorium
Teacher Institute

KENDALL/HUNT PUBLISHING COMPANY
4050 Westmark Drive   Dubuque, Iowa 52002

Project Manager: Kurt Feichtmeir

Managing Editor: Judith Brand

Developmental Editor: Eric Engles

Designer: David Barker

Editorial Production Manager:
  Ellyn Hament

Production Editor: Michael Matz

Illustrator: Marijo Racciatti

Photo Researcher: Megan Bury

Production Assistants: Moira McGowan,
  Wendy Hakoda

Human Body Explorations was developed by the Teacher Institute, a part of the Exploratorium Regional Science Resource Center, which is funded by the California Department of Education. The Exploratorium also gratefully acknowledges the Howard Hughes Medical Institute for its support of the Exploratorium Teacher Institute's new work in the life sciences.

 BE CAREFUL! The explorations in this work were designed with safety and success in mind. But even the simplest activity or the most common materials could be harmful when mishandled or misused. Use common sense whenever you're exploring or experimenting.

Contents

The Explorations

Part 1: Your Secret Body

Investigations of hidden processes and phenomena

Part 2: Your Observable Body

Investigations of perceivable processes and phenomena

Appendix

About *Human Body Explorations*

Nothing is more fascinating than the human body! We all have one, and we're intimately familiar with what it can do. But why and how does it do the things it does? The explorations in this book will lead to a better understanding of many of the intriguing and mysterious aspects of the body, both macroscopic and microscopic. All that's needed are a few simple tools, curiosity, and in some cases a little help from others.

Everyone is a learner, and we have written the explorations in this book to reflect that fact. The explorations are successful in the classroom—but most can be done outside the classroom equally well. Many can be conducted by a curious individual. For others, a partner or a few other co-explorers are needed.

The explorations provide experience in asking questions that can be answered through scientific investigation. They ask an explorer to gather, analyze, and interpret data using a variety of simple tools and techniques, and guide the process of developing explanations, predictions, and models using the evidence that's generated. Making connections between evidence and explanation develops critical thinking skills and builds an excellent foundation for further independent inquiry.

With a few exceptions, the materials needed for the explorations are available in a grocery store or pharmacy at little cost, and we give detailed instructions on preparation and setup. We provide extensive scientific background and explanations, and there's a list of additional resources in the back of the book. We've also included useful tips and ideas for inquiry that can be used to modify the explorations to suit individual needs and goals.

How to Use This Book

Some of the explorations need someone to fill the role of facilitator. The facilitator may prepare materials in advance, guide and coordinate the activities of a group of learners, or "explorers," keep track of information to be revealed at the conclusion of the activity, and help learners make connections between their results or observations and the human body. The facilitator need not be a teacher, but he or she may need to be someone other than the learner or group of learners. In many of the explorations, however, having a facilitator is optional, or learners can, in effect, act as their own facilitators.

The first part of each exploration, containing the what-to-do steps that make up the activity itself, is directed to the explorer. The other three parts of each exploration, Preparation and Setup, After the Exploration, and The Basics and Beyond, are directed to the facilitator. See Anatomy of an Exploration for a detailed description of each of these sections.

How these sections are used depends, of course, on your situation. If you are a teacher using the explorations in the classroom, you may want to duplicate the activity pages for the explorers in the class and use the information in the other three parts to inform your role as facilitator. A parent or other adult facilitator may choose to operate in a similar manner. If you want to carry out the explorations on your own, you will need to choose those that don't require co-explorers or separate facilitators, and then use all parts of the exploration in the way that seems best.

When you are taking on the role of facilitator, you will have many options concerning when and how to present information to explorers to guide their discussion and discovery. Some explorations can be effective learning experiences with only minimal guidance from the facilitator, while others are best carried out with more extensive facilitator involvement. One important choice involves the use of the Background information presented in The Basics and Beyond—facilitators may want to pass along some or all of this information to explorers before they begin the activity.

Facilitators should be aware of how to treat explorers' results and observations. Unexpected results are sometimes obtained that are not necessarily due to error or poor technique. We recommend using any unexpected results as an opportunity for inquiry. Try to determine the reason for the discrepancy! The actual reason may not be discovered, but the process of trying to figure something out is an important part of science.

In the Preparation and Setup section, facilitators are provided with a suggested group size, which can range from one to many. In most cases, the group size can be varied without any significant modification of the activity. However, some of the explorations are written with a particular number of explorers in mind. Several, for example, require at least two explorers working together, and one can be done only with a group of about a dozen or more.

Remember that this book is a starting point for exploration of the human body, not a rigid lesson plan. We encourage you to modify each exploration in any way you see fit, and to exercise your creativity and curiosity.

We hope that you have as much fun and learn as much as we did by diving into these explorations. Rather than solving all of the body's mysteries for you, we hope we stimulate your spirit of inquiry so that you'll want to question and explore even more!

Anatomy of an Exploration

The four parts of an exploration are described below. How you use these parts, and in what order, depends on your role in the exploration and on your own preferences and goals.

1. The Activity

Things You Will Need Provides a list of everything an explorer needs to conduct the investigation. The items listed are the things that are actually used by the explorer; some of them may need to be prepared in advance from other materials, sometimes by someone acting as facilitator.

To Do and Notice Gives step-by-step instructions for conducting the investigation, including suggestions to facilitate data collecting and organization. Caution icons in this section point out potential hazards and steps that may require careful attention.

Analyzing Data and Drawing Conclusions Appears when specific and discrete data are gathered and helps explorers analyze and interpret their data.

Interpreting Observations Appears when the activity largely elicits observations recorded in words and helps explorers draw conclusions from what they've observed.

Displaying Data Appears when a graph would be useful and encourages the explorer to display the data in graphic form for easier interpretation and clearer communication of results.

2. Preparation and Setup

Materials Lists "for the whole group" those items that can be shared by explorers (such as balances) and raw materials used in the preparation of the hands-on materials. Hands-on items used directly in the exploration are listed under "for each pair or small group" or "for each explorer."

Management Gives an approximate amount of time needed to conduct the activity, an estimated length of time needed to prepare materials (not including the time needed to purchase or "round up" materials), and a suggested group size.

TIPS! Offers an idea or ideas for tailoring the exploration for a particular group, or for optimizing the learning experience.

Activity Overview Provides a very brief summary of the activity.

Concepts Lists the major points of science content involved in the exploration.

Preparation Provides detailed instructions for preparing materials.

Questions for Getting Started Suggests questions to help access existing knowledge that may be useful in conducting the exploration or interpreting results.

3. After the Exploration

Expected Results Describes "typical" results for an investigation, assuming that it was conducted as written.

What's Going On? Explains the scientific phenomena and principles underlying the exploration.

Discussion Questions Poses post-exploration questions that stimulate critical thinking skills and connect the explorations to day-to-day experiences.

Going Further: Ideas for Inquiry Suggests starting points for further exploration.

4. The Basics and Beyond

Background Provides a scientific context for understanding the purpose of the exploration and interpreting the results.

Tidbits Imparts fascinating facts related to the exploration.

Before You Begin

Potential hazards, cautions, and alternatives

Safety Precautions

We've designed these explorations with safety and success in mind. But even the simplest activity and the most common materials can be harmful when mishandled or misused. Use common sense whenever you're exploring or experimenting.

We have used a CAUTION icon ⚠ and an explanatory note to draw your attention to any steps for which extra care should be taken.

Ingesting Materials

A few of the explorations in this book require tasting or smelling substances. If you are a teacher or other group facilitator, be sure to check the rules of your organization regarding liability and parental permission for ingesting substances before asking anyone to participate in an exploration that involves tasting or smelling.

Some individuals may be unable to participate in a tasting or smelling activity due to dietary, medical, or other restrictions. We encourage the creation of alternative roles for those who cannot, or do not wish to, taste or smell the suggested materials. In a group situation, for example, those who cannot directly participate may be given the role of an assistant who passes out materials or gathers and records data.

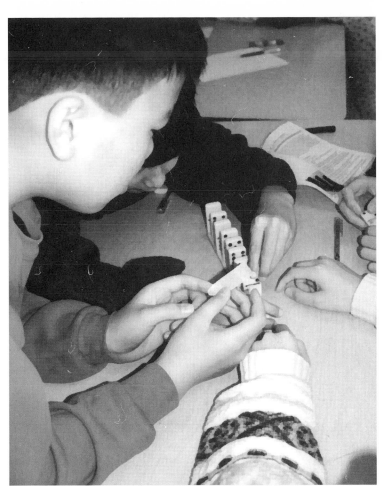

Part 1
Your Secret Body

Explorer's Guide

Naked Egg

Put de-shelled eggs in different fluids and watch them swell and shrink

All of the trillions of cells in your body are like busy sea ports, with materials coming in and going out. Use a giant cell—a de-shelled chicken egg—to explore the comings and goings of cellular substances.

Caution:
Bacterial contamination of eggs is relatively common. Avoid touching your mouth when you are handling the eggs, and wash your hands thoroughly after each session. It's also wise to wear rubber or latex gloves when you handle the eggs.

Things You Will Need

- ▲ several de-shelled chicken eggs
- ▲ access to a balance
- ▲ several substances in which to soak the eggs, such as distilled water, saltwater solutions, water mixed with food coloring, and corn syrup
- ▲ containers in which to hold the soaking eggs
- ▲ tape and marker for labeling containers
- ▲ rubber or latex gloves for handling eggs (optional)
- ▲ paper for recording data

To Do and Notice

You will be soaking eggs in several different substances, each of which will affect its egg in a different way. Each substance is called a treatment. The choice of treatments is up to you.

First Day

❶ Determine the treatments you will use on your eggs. For each treatment, predict what will happen to the egg. Record your predictions.

❷ Find the mass of one of the de-shelled eggs using a balance. Record the mass. Handle the de-shelled egg gently.

❸ Place the egg in a labeled treatment container. Cover it with your chosen treatment. If the egg floats, you may use something to hold it down.

❹ Repeat steps 2 and 3 for each of the remaining treatments.

❺ Place the treatment containers in a place where they can sit for at least a day at room temperature.

❻ Observe any changes that occur in the eggs during the first hour or so of soaking and record your observations.

Second Day

❶ Observe any changes in the color, size, or shape of your experimental eggs. Record your observations.

❷ Find and record the mass of each experimental egg.

❸ Calculate the percentage change in mass for each egg by dividing the final mass of the egg by the starting mass and multiplying by 100.

Analyzing Data and Drawing Conclusions

How did each egg change? Did its mass increase or decrease? Do you see anything in common among the treatments that enlarged their eggs? Among the treatments that shrunk their eggs?

Facilitator's Guide
Naked Egg

Materials

for the whole group

▲ chicken eggs (each small group will need several)

▲ large containers with lids to hold large numbers of eggs for de-shelling

▲ white vinegar

▲ beakers or cups to hold eggs during treatments

▲ tape and markers for labeling containers

▲ balance

▲ a variety of substances for treating the eggs, such as distilled water, salt solutions of various concentrations, solutions of food coloring, and corn syrup (undiluted)

▲ latex or rubber gloves

▲ paper for recording data

Management

▲ Amount of time for the activity: 20–30 minutes for each of two days

▲ Preparation time: a few minutes to gather supplies (not including de-shelling of eggs, which must begin 24 to 48 hours ahead of time)

▲ Group size: 1–3+ (depends on the number of eggs available)

Preparation and Setup

Activity Overview

Use de-shelled chicken eggs as models for investigating diffusion and osmosis across plasma membranes.

Concepts

❯ Cells are bounded by plasma membranes.

❯ Plasma membranes are selectively permeable, allowing some substances to pass through freely and restricting the transit of other substances.

❯ Particles tend to move from an area of higher concentration to an area of lower concentration because of random molecular motion; this movement is called diffusion.

❯ Osmosis is the diffusion of water across a selectively permeable membrane.

Preparation

❶ De-shell the eggs: Place eggs in a large container so that they are not touching. Add vinegar to cover the eggs. Cover the container. Allow the eggs to sit for 24 to 48 hours, with one change of vinegar. (The more vinegar you use, the faster the reaction occurs.) Rinse the eggs in water to remove any traces of softened shell. Refrigerate the eggs until used.

❷ Obtain ready-made treatment substances, such as distilled water and corn syrup.

❸ Prepare other treatment substances: Make salt solutions by dissolving different amounts of table salt in containers of water (e.g., 100 g, 200 g, and 300 g of NaCl per liter). Make solutions of food coloring by adding a few drops of each color to a container of water.

Questions for Getting Started

❯ What happens if you put a single drop of food coloring in a beaker of water? Why?

❯ What happens to your fingertips if you have your hands in water for a long period of time? Why do you think this happens?

After the Exploration

Expected Results

In general, the most dramatic changes in the mass, color, and shape of the eggs will occur within the first 24 hours of the experiment. Eggs in corn syrup will have lost considerable mass and have the appearance of flabby sacks. Eggs in distilled water will gain mass and appear dramatically swollen. Eggs in dilute salt solutions will gain mass, and those in very concentrated solutions will lose mass. Eggs in food coloring will take up the color they are treated with.

What's Going On?

The de-shelled eggs are good models of human cells. After the eggshell is removed, a white membrane remains. (It's actually two membranes, but they're held tightly together.) This membrane, like those of human cells, is selectively permeable, and the entire egg is a single cell.

Substances that can pass easily through the membrane of the egg will follow the principle of diffusion: they will move from the side of the membrane where they are at higher concentration to the side of the membrane where they are at lower concentration (see Figures 1A and 1B). This movement will continue until the concentrations on both sides of the membrane are equal.

Water is one substance to which the egg's membrane is permeable. (The movement of water across a membrane is a special case of diffusion called osmosis.) When an egg is soaked in a solution in which the concentration of water is lower than that inside the egg, water moves from the egg, across the membrane, and into the solution (see Figure 2). As a result, the egg loses mass and may end up looking like a flabby bag. This is what occurs when an egg is treated in corn syrup.

When an egg is treated with distilled water or a not-too-concentrated salt solution, the concentration of water is higher outside the egg, so water moves into the egg and increases its mass.

The egg's membrane is also permeable to food-coloring particles. When an egg is treated in a solution of food coloring, the concentration of food-coloring particles is higher outside the egg, so particles diffuse into the egg and give it color. (If you cut open the colored egg, you will note that some of the dye has bound to the egg membranes, due to interacting charges between the food coloring particles and the membrane components.)

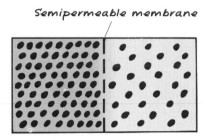

Ⓐ *Before diffusion*

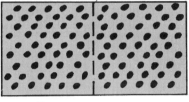

Ⓑ *After diffusion*

Figures 1A and 1B: A substance before and after it undergoes diffusion

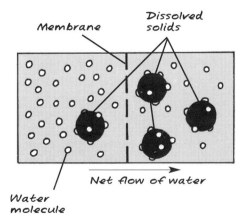

Figure 2: The diffusion of water across a membrane, a process called osmosis

The plasma membranes of our cells behave much like those of the eggs. Water, oxygen, and nutrients must pass through the plasma membrane into our cells, and wastes must leave. Oxygen diffuses into red blood cells in our lungs, and they transport the oxygen to our tissues, where the oxygen diffuses into other cells. Through osmosis, water in the stomach moves into the bloodstream. Without sufficient water to carry out essential bodily functions, our cells would shrivel up and die, eventually killing us.

Discussion Questions

❶ The lactose molecule is large and cannot pass through the lining of the large intestine like water can. When lactose-intolerant people eat dairy products, one of the resulting symptoms is watery stool. Considering the results of this exploration, can you explain why this occurs?

❷ When you're in fresh water for a long time, your fingers and toes get puffy because they absorb water. What do you think will occur when you swim for a long time in the ocean?

❸ Why was it important to calculate the percentage change in mass of each egg?

Going Further: Ideas for Inquiry

❯ Put an egg colored by food coloring into distilled water. What happens after a night of soaking, and why? Predict what will happen if you take an egg treated in corn syrup and soak it overnight. Do the experiment and explain your results.

❯ Leave the eggs in their treatments for a week. How do their masses change over time? Dissect the eggs after they sit for a week and see if there are any changes in the yolk.

❯ Dextrose is the major sugar in corn syrup. Do you think that dextrose diffused into the corn-syrup-treated eggs? Perform Benedict's test (see the activity "How Sweet It Is," page 37) to find out.

❯ If you soak a series of eggs in different concentrations of food coloring, do you think there will be differences in their appearance after one day? Do the experiment and find out.

The Basics and Beyond

Background

Every cell of our bodies is enclosed in a plasma membrane, a complex multilayered boundary between the cell contents and the surrounding extracellular fluid. These membranes play a major role in cell processes and homeostasis by controlling what passes through them. One of the most important characteristics of plasma membranes is their selective permeability: Water, small ions, small uncharged particles, and hydrophobic (lipid-soluble) molecules cross the plasma membrane easily through the process of diffusion, but large molecules can move through the plasma membrane only through special, energy-expending processes.

The movement of substances across human plasma membranes can be dramatically modeled using de-shelled chicken eggs, which are giant single cells.

Tidbits

❭ Eggshell is composed of calcium carbonate. When it is submerged in vinegar (5% acetic acid) the calcium carbonate reacts with the acetic acid:

$$CaCO_3 + 2CH_3CO_2H \rightarrow Ca^{++} + H_2CO_3 + 2CH_3CO_2^-$$

calcium carbonate   acetic acid   carbonic acid   acetate

The carbonic acid formed in this way dissociates rapidly:

$$H_2CO_3 \rightarrow H_2O + CO_2$$

The bubbles that develop after you cover the eggs with vinegar are due to the carbon dioxide produced as a by-product of the reaction of the eggshell with the vinegar.

❭ Modified neurons called osmoreceptors keep tabs on the concentration of water in the blood. When the concentration falls below a certain level, the osmoreceptors send signals to the brain that result in the sensation of thirst.

❭ The average size of a human ovum (egg) is 0.013 cm.

Explorer's Guide
Cellular Soap Opera

Soap films can behave like cell membranes

Every cell in your body needs to take in nutrients, oxygen, and raw materials and to export wastes and other substances. But it's not just a random traffic jam! The cell membrane regulates what comes in and goes out. Use a soap film to simulate a plasma membrane, and explore the ins and outs of cellular traffic.

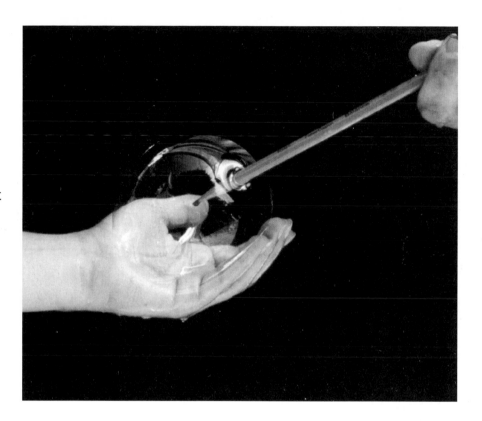

Things You Will Need

▲ bubble solution
▲ water
▲ 2 pieces of string, 1 long and 1 short
▲ a drinking straw
▲ scissors
▲ aluminum pie pan or similar container
▲ 2 film cans, with tops and bottoms removed
▲ sheet of black construction paper

To Do and Notice

It is easiest to do this activity with at least two people. One person can make the soap film and hold the handle, while the other person explores how the film behaves.

❶ Cut the straw in half with the scissors.

❷ Thread the longer string through the two half-straws and tie the ends together to make a loop. Cut the excess string from the ends of the knot. Move the string through the half-straws so that the knot is hidden inside one of the straws. This is your bubble frame.

❸ Create a handle for the frame by threading the shorter string through one of the straws and tying the ends together. An easy way to get the string through the straw is to tie it to the string loop you made in the previous step and then pull the loop to bring the tied end through one of the straws. Then untie the knot and make the handle. The frame and handle should look something like the drawing in Figure 1.

❹ Fill the pie pan with the soap solution, at least 2 cm deep.

❺ Shape the bubble frame into a rectangle (as shown in Figure 1). Holding the frame by the handle, immerse the entire frame in the bubble solution.

❻ Lift the frame up by the handle until the bottom of the frame is slightly out of the bubble solution and the half-straws are parallel to the table top. You should have a rectangular soap film between the two half-straws. If there isn't a soap film, try immersing and lifting the frame again.

❼ Hold the soap film in front of a piece of black construction paper or other black material. Carefully observe the surface of the film. Blow gently on the film and watch what happens.

Repeat steps 5 and 6 if the soap film pops while you are completing the steps below.

❽ Wet your finger in the bubble solution. Gently poke it through the soap film. What happens? Can you move your finger around in the film? Now wet your finger in plain water and poke it into the film. What happens?

❾ Try gently poking a dry finger through the soap film. What happens now?

❿ Make a new film on the frame. Roll a film can (with the top and bottom removed) in the bubble solution to coat the surfaces of the can. Grasp the film can near one end and remove it from the solution. If films have formed across the openings of the can, pop them. Insert one end of the film can through the soap film on the frame. If the film pops, make another and try again.

⓫ When you successfully insert a bubble-solution-coated film can through the soap film, leave the can in this position and have your partner or someone else pass an object (such as a pencil) through the openings in the can, from one side of the film to the other. Can you move the film can around in the soap film?

⓬ Try putting a dry film can through the soap film.

Analyzing Data and Drawing Conclusions

Based on your observations, what conditions allow objects to pass through the soap film without popping it? What conditions cause the film to pop? Do you think the flexibility of the film influences its ability to resist popping? Why or why not?

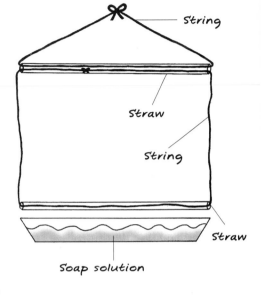

Figure 1: A completed
soap film frame

Facilitator's Guide
Cellular Soap Opera

Materials

for the whole group

▲ liquid dishwashing detergent*

▲ glycerin*

▲ water

*commercial bubble solution can substitute for these materials

for each small group

▲ a drinking straw

▲ 2 pieces of string, 1 a bit more than twice the length of the straw, the second about 1.5 times the straw length

▲ scissors

▲ an aluminum pie pan or similar container

▲ 2 film cans with tops and bottoms removed (see Preparation)

▲ a sheet of black construction paper

Management

▲ Amount of time for the activity: 20–30 minutes

▲ Preparation time: 15 minutes

▲ Group size: 2 (or more)

TIPS!

● This activity can be done with "Naked Egg" (page 11) to give a complete lesson on plasma membrane structure and function.

● You can make larger bubble frames by using whole straws and scaling up the lengths of the string and the size of the bubble solution containers.

Preparation and Setup

Activity Overview

Explore the properties of soap films and relate them to the properties of plasma membranes and the mechanics of transport across membranes.

Concepts

❯ Cells need to import some materials, such as oxygen and nutrients, and export others, such as wastes.

❯ At the boundary of every cell is a plasma membrane that regulates what is transported into and out of the cell.

❯ The plasma membrane is a mosaic of proteins inserted into a fluid bilayer of phospholipids. The proteins float laterally in the membrane.

❯ Substances most like the phospholipids in the membrane easily pass through it, as do very small molecules. Substances unlike the membrane, and very large molecules, can cross the plasma membrane only with assistance from the protein "channels."

Preparation

❶ Purchase a large quantity of commercial bubble solution or make your own. To make your own, obtain dish detergent and glycerin. Mix ⅔ cup of detergent and 1 tablespoon glycerin per gallon of water. Let the solution age at least overnight for the longest-lasting bubbles.

❷ Cut the bottoms off of the film cans. Use a sharp knife or single-edge razor blade to pierce the side near the bottom, then cut the bottoms off using sharp scissors.

Caution: Be careful when using sharp instruments.

Questions for Getting Started

❯ What types of substances do human beings need to take in to their bodies and eliminate from their bodies? Do our individual cells need to do similar things?

❯ How does the oxygen collected by your lungs enter blood cells? Where do the blood cells take the oxygen, and what happens when they give up the oxygen?

After the Exploration

Expected Results

When viewed against a black sheet of paper, it is obvious that the soap film is moving, not static, and that its colors are constantly changing. When you gently blow on it, the film stretches outward and appears very flexible. A finger coated with soap solution or water is easily inserted through the film and can be moved around. A film can coated with bubble solution can also be inserted through the soap film, creating a "tunnel" through which objects can be passed. Trying to penetrate the soap film with a dry finger or dry film can pops the soap film.

What's Going On?

The soap film is a "water sandwich"—a layer of water positioned between two layers of soap (or detergent) molecules. The hydrophilic heads of the soap molecules point inward toward the water layer, and the hydrophobic tails of the soap molecules point toward the outside of the film, in contact with the air (see Figure 2).

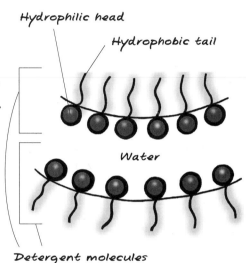

Figure 2: Soap film structure

The surface tension that causes bubbles, or bubble films, is due to the tendency of water, through hydrogen bonding, to minimize its surface area. When a finger, film can, or other object is wetted with bubble solution and inserted through the soap film, the film remains in contact with a like solution, continues to minimize its surface area, and doesn't burst. Likewise, with a water-coated object, the tendency of water to minimize its surface area causes the film to stretch at the point of entry but not burst. A dry object, however, mechanically sheers the film.

Plasma membranes are similar to soap films in several respects. To begin with, they are both bilayered structures, formed by molecules with hydrophilic and hydrophobic ends (compare Figure 2 on this page with Figure 3, page 22). Second, both allow objects to move laterally within them—moving the film can around in the soap film models the way that proteins are able to move around within the plasma membrane. Third, plasma membranes and soap films are both flexible, nonrigid structures.

In addition, plasma membranes and soap films are both selectively permeable. Plasma membranes allow hydrophobic substances to pass through them, much like the soap film allows the coated finger to pass through it, because hydrophobic substances are highly soluble in the lipid bilayer. Among polar (partially charged) molecules, only small ones such as H_2O and CO_2 can easily pass through the spaces between the phospholipids. Very large polar molecules (such as glucose) and fully-charged ions such as Na^+ and K^+ require special transport processes to cross the membrane. These substances are similar to the dry finger inserted in the soap film—they cannot pass through without special modifications. (One major difference between soap films and plasma membranes is that plasma membranes do not "pop" when confronted with an unlike substance!)

Finally, both plasma membranes and soap films (with appropriate modification) can allow the passage of large or unlike substances. Substances that can't cross the plasma membrane on their own are transported through special processes that involve the proteins embedded in the plasma membrane. In some cases, the proteins provide channels or tunnels for the passage of molecules or ions. The wet film cans inserted into the soap film are much like these protein channels.

The swirling colors you can see in the soap film are a characteristic of soap films not shared by plasma membranes. The changing colors are an example of iridescence, which is caused by interference between the light waves reflecting off the back surface of the soap film and those reflecting off the front surface. The slight offset between these two sets of light waves is approximately equal to a wavelength of light, and so when they are combined, some wavelengths (i.e., colors) of light are cancelled out while others are strengthened. The colors change because the thickness of the soap film changes, changing the amount of offset between the two sets of light waves.

Discussion Questions

❶ Can you think of any examples of water moving across a membrane?

❷ What roles do diffusion and osmosis play in the transport of materials across a plasma membrane?

Going Further: Ideas for Inquiry

❯ Coat a finger with a different type of fluid (for example, vegetable oil or rubbing alcohol) and see if you can penetrate the film without popping it. Try it several times with different fluids. What do the fluids that work seem to have in common?

❯ Obtain a culture of the single-celled protozoan *Paramecium*. While observing it under a microscope, feed it some yeast cells. How does the organism bring in its food across its plasma membrane?

The Basics and Beyond

Background

The membranes surrounding cells are called plasma membranes. They are made of two layers of phospholipid molecules, with each molecule having a hydrophilic (water-loving) "head" and a hydrophobic (water-hating) "tail." In each layer, the hydrophobic "tails" of the phospholipids point inward; the hydrophilic "heads" point outward, in contact with the watery environments inside and outside of the cell (see Figure 3). This bilayer structure is studded with proteins. The proteins move laterally within the membrane, forming what is called a "fluid mosaic."

Nutrients, respiratory gases, wastes, and inorganic ions must all pass through the membrane on their way into or out of the cell. The unique structure of the plasma membrane allows it to be selectively permeable: some substances can easily enter and exit the cell through the plasma membrane, while others cannot pass through without assistance from the embedded proteins.

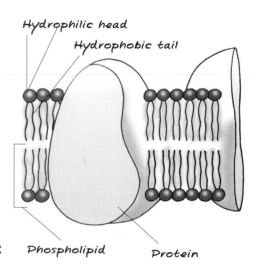

Figure 3:
Plasma membrane structure

Tidbits

❯ The disease cystic fibrosis is a genetically inherited disorder caused by a defect in a protein that acts as a channel for chloride ions to pass through the plasma membrane of certain types of cells. Most affected are cells in the sweat ducts and respiratory tract. Because chloride ions aren't transported appropriately, thick plugs of mucus block the pulmonary airways. Affected individuals may develop recurrent bacterial infections.

❯ After a nerve cell has fired, it has a refractory period during which it cannot fire again (see the activity "The Domino Effect," page 75). During the refractory period, the cell is using a sodium-potassium pump to reset the initial concentration of sodium and potassium ions in the cell. This "pump" is made up of transport proteins embedded in the plasma membrane that move the potassium ions into the cell and the sodium ions out of the cell.

Explorer's Guide
Acid in Your Stomach

Find out which antacid is most effective

Have you ever eaten too much pizza and gotten a stomach ache? Maybe you took an antacid to help you to feel better. But which one should you choose? Get beyond the hype of commercials to discover which one really neutralizes acid the most effectively.

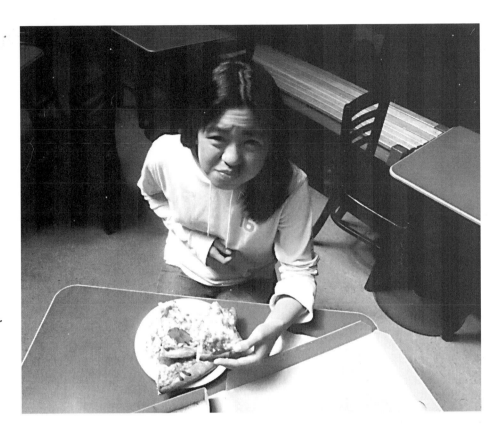

⚠

Caution:
Don't eat or drink anything in this experiment.

Things You Will Need

- ▲ vinegar
- ▲ 25 mL or larger graduated cylinder
- ▲ universal pH paper
- ▲ mortar and pestle or similar crushing device
- ▲ 4 beakers or cups, 50 mL volume or larger
- ▲ several coffee stirrers or similar stirring devices
- ▲ ½-teaspoon, teaspoon, and tablespoon measuring spoons
- ▲ baking soda and 3 other antacids with different active ingredients
- ▲ access to a clock or watch with a second hand
- ▲ paper for recording data

To Do and Notice

❶ Read the labels of the antacids and baking soda to find the lowest recommended dosage for each. Get a sheet of paper on which to record data from the experiment.

❷ Set out 4 cups and pour 25 mL of vinegar into each one. (Vinegar is 5% acetic acid, and represents the acid in your stomach.)

❸ Use the pH paper and its color scale to find the pH of the vinegar. Record the pH.

❹ Choose one antacid. Add its lowest recommended single dose to the cup of vinegar. If it is a tablet, crush it first with a mortar and pestle. **Important:** When you use baking soda, add it directly to the vinegar; do not dilute it first as the package suggests.

❺ Mix the vinegar and antacid thoroughly with a stirring device and wait 1 minute. Test and record the pH. Record any observations of activity in the cup.

❻ Repeat steps 4 and 5 for the three other antacids. Be sure to use a fresh cup of vinegar and clean stirrer each time. Clean the mortar and pestle (and measuring spoon, if used) between each use.

Analyzing Data and Drawing Conclusions

According to your results, which antacid does the best job of raising the pH of vinegar? Do you think this antacid will work best in your stomach, too?

Displaying Data

Make a bar graph that shows how much each antacid raised the pH of vinegar.

very acidic	0	
	1	
	2	gastric juice
	3	
	4	soda water
	5	black coffee
	6	milk
neutral	7	pure water
	8	seawater
	9	baking soda
	10	
	11	ammonia
	12	
	13	
very alkaline	14	

The pH Scale

Facilitator's Guide

Acid in Your Stomach

Materials

for each pair

▲ 100 mL vinegar

▲ 25 mL or larger graduated cylinder

▲ universal pH paper, range 0–14 in units of 1.0

▲ mortar and pestle or similar crushing device

▲ 4 beakers or cups, 50 mL volume or larger

▲ coffee stirrers or similar stirring devices

▲ ½-teaspoon, teaspoon, and tablespoon measuring spoons

▲ baking soda and 3 other antacids with different active ingredients; e.g., Tums or Rolaids, Mylanta or milk of magnesia, Alka Seltzer

▲ access to a clock or watch with a second hand

▲ paper for recording data

Management

▲ Amount of time for the activity: 30–40 minutes

▲ Preparation time: 10 minutes to set out materials

▲ Group size: 2

Preparation and Setup

Activity Overview

Test the ability of different antacids to raise the pH of vinegar and in this way learn which antacids may be best at neutralizing stomach acid.

Concepts

❭ The pH scale expresses a measurement of the acidity or alkalinity of a fluid.

❭ Our stomachs produce hydrochloric acid, which is very acidic.

❭ Sometimes our stomachs over-produce acid, or we become extra-sensitive to our stomach acid, which causes acid indigestion.

❭ Products called antacids can neutralize excess acid, and they vary in their ability to do so.

Preparation

None, except for obtaining materials. Store brands of antacids can be substituted for national brands. Be sure to use antacids and not products that block the production of stomach acid. Participants can bring assorted antacids from home to keep costs down and increase the number of available antacid products.

Questions for Getting Started

❭ Have you heard of pH before? In what context?

❭ Can you give some examples of acids and bases?

❭ What is the purpose of the acid in your stomach?

TIPS!

● This activity can be completed in less time if you pre-measure the vinegar into the cups; also, each pair can test only one antacid and share the results with other pairs.

● Demonstrate how to use the pH paper and color key.

After the Exploration

Expected Results

Baking soda (sodium bicarbonate) is likely to be most effective in raising the pH of vinegar. (This doesn't mean it is the best antacid to take: many people already have too much sodium in their diets.)

When antacids containing either sodium bicarbonate or calcium carbonate are added to the vinegar, bubbles of gas should be observed (in both cases the gas is carbon dioxide).

The vinegar in a cup is only a simulation of the stomach's gastric juices. Any conclusion about the effectiveness of the antacids in the human body based on the results of the experiment is an inference.

What's Going On?

White vinegar is about 5% acetic acid, CH_3COOH. It has a pH of about 3, not quite as acidic as gastric juice. Acetic acid is an acid because one of its hydrogen atoms is easily released into solution as a hydrogen ion.

The different antacids used in this investigation raise the pH of vinegar in different ways, depending on their active ingredients. In each antacid, the "active ingredient" is a particular base.

Sodium bicarbonate (Alka Seltzer®, baking soda) raises the pH of vinegar by tying up hydrogen ions. It ionizes into sodium ions and bicarbonate ions, and the bicarbonate ions combine with hydrogen ions to form carbonic acid. Some of the carbonic acid dissociates to form water and carbon dioxide, and some of this carbon dioxide bubbles out of the solution. Overall, the carbonic acid stays in equilibrium with water and carbon dioxide on the one hand, and with bicarbonate ions and hydrogen ions on the other; but enough hydrogen ions are tied up in both the carbonic acid and the water to raise the pH of the solution.

$$NaHCO_3 \rightarrow Na^+ + HCO_3^- \qquad HCO_3^- + H^+ \leftrightarrow H_2CO_3 \leftrightarrow H_2O + CO_2$$

sodium bicarbonate   carbonic acid

This mechanism for raising pH does not by itself explain why sodium bicarbonate is usually found to be most effective in this activity. The amount of active ingredient is much larger in baking soda (nearly pure sodium bicarbonate) than it is in the other products. The other products contain inactive ingredients—as you can see from reading the product labels—that have no effect on pH.

Calcium carbonate (Tums®) raises the pH of the vinegar in much the same way as sodium bicarbonate. It ionizes into calcium ions and carbonate ions, and the carbonate ions bond with hydrogen ions to form carbonic acid, which forms—and stays in equilibrium with—water and carbon dioxide:

$$CaCO_3 \rightarrow Ca^{2+} + CO_3^{2-} \qquad CO_3^{2-} + 2H^+ \leftrightarrow H_2CO_3 \leftrightarrow H_2O + CO_2$$

calcium carbonate   carbonic acid

Aluminum hydroxide (Mylanta®) and magnesium hydroxide (Mylanta, milk of magnesia) raise the pH of the vinegar by contributing hydroxide ions, which combine with hydrogen ions to produce water:

$$Al(OH)_3 \rightarrow Al^{3+} + 3OH^-$$

aluminum hydroxide

$$Mg(OH)_2 \rightarrow Mg^{2+} + 2OH^- \qquad OH^- + H^+ \leftrightarrow H_2O$$

magnesium hydroxide

Discussion Questions

❶ Did you notice any bubbling or foaming with any of the antacids? Which ones? What do they have in their ingredients that the other antacids do not? Do you think this could be the cause of the bubbling? If you take baking soda for an upset stomach, what do you suppose happens to all of the gas that is produced?

❷ How do you think your results might differ if you use the same amount of antacid for each trial, rather than the recommended dosage?

❸ The pH of our stomachs is normally very acidic. Why do you think this is so?

❹ Many commercials and advertisements for products such as shampoo, soap, and deodorant say that the products are "pH balanced." What do you suppose this means and why would it be important?

Going Further: Ideas for Inquiry

❯ Find out more about the role of stomach acid in digestion, and how the stomach protects itself from the acid.

❯ Calculate the cost per dose of each antacid, the frequency of doses needed, and so on, to discover which antacid may be the best value for the money.

❯ Calculate the hydrogen ion concentrations and hydroxide ion concentrations associated with the different pHs measured during the activity. Use the following equations (the square brackets [ ] indicate concentration in moles per liter).

$$pH = - \log [H^+]$$
in pure water (pH = 7), $[H^+] = 10^{-7}$ M; $[OH^-] = 10^{-7}$ M
in any solution, $[H^+] [OH^-] = 10^{-14}$ M

The Basics and Beyond

Background

Water solutions vary in their relative concentration of hydrogen ions (H^+) and hydroxide ions (OH^-). When hydrogen ions predominate, the solution is acidic; when hydroxide ions predominate, the solution is alkaline (basic). The acidity or alkalinity of a solution is measured with the pH scale, which goes from 0 to 14 (see page 24). A pH less than 7 indicates acidity; a pH greater than 7 indicates alkalinity; a pH of 7 is neutral. The pH of a solution is the negative logarithm of its hydrogen ion concentration.

Compounds that can add hydrogen ions to a solution are called acids; those that can reduce the concentration of hydrogen ions are called bases. Adding a base to an acid solution raises its pH, and adding an acid to a basic solution lowers its pH.

Our stomachs produce hydrochloric acid (HCl) to aid digestion. The acid helps begin to break down the protein in food, and it also helps digestive enzymes do their work. The pH of the gastric juices in the stomach is typically about pH 2. Normal amounts of HCl don't bother us, in part because the cells of the stomach are protected by a layer of mucus. But stress or spicy food may increase the stomach's sensitivity to acid or cause the stomach to produce more acid than it needs, resulting in discomfort.

Over-the-counter antacids are commonly used to combat occasional excess stomach acid. They all contain bases that work to neutralize stomach acid. But these bases vary in chemical structure and effectiveness.

Tidbits

❯ A normal stomach produces 2–3 liters of acidic gastric juice every day.

❯ Although the stomach's mucous layer does a good job of protecting the cells lining the stomach, those cells that do get damaged are shed and rapidly replaced. About a half-million cells are replaced every minute, which means that the entire stomach lining is replaced every 3 days.

Explorer's Guide
How Much Do You C?

*Find out how much
vitamin C a drink contains*

Bleeding gums and bruised
skin are just two symptoms
of vitamin C deficiency. Do
you have enough of this
important vitamin in your
diet to avoid such a fate?
Do this experiment and learn
more about vitamin C!

Things You Will Need

▲ about 75 mL vitamin C standard solution
▲ about 25 mL 1% starch solution
▲ 1 10-mL graduated cylinder
▲ 1 50- or 100-mL graduated cylinder
▲ 1 100-mL or larger beaker or flask
▲ pipette or dropper calibrated to 1 mL
▲ 2 medicine droppers
▲ potato slice or bread slice
▲ water
▲ bottle of iodine
▲ a clock with a second hand
▲ drinks for testing
▲ paper for recording data

To Do and Notice
This activity works best with a facilitator.

Reacting Starch with Iodine

❶ Add a drop of iodine to the surface of a slice of potato or bread. Wait for a few seconds. What happens? (Label the dropper "iodine" and use this dropper only for iodine throughout the activity.)

❷ Using the 1-mL calibrated pipette or dropper, place 10 drops of starch solution in one of the cylinders. Add a drop of iodine and wait a few seconds. What happens? (Keep the pipette for use only with the starch solution throughout the activity. Dispose of the solution in the cylinder and rinse the cylinder.)

❸ Place 10 drops of the vitamin C standard solution in one of the cylinders. Add a drop of iodine and wait a few seconds. What happens? (Dispose of the solution and rinse out the dropper and cylinder.)

You probably observed that the iodine changed from a reddish-brown color to blue-black as it interacted with the starch solution. The same color reaction occurs with the potato or bread, but not with the vitamin C solution. What does this suggest about the makeup of potatoes and bread? The color reaction is specific for starch—a color change you'll be watching for in this exploration. Because the vitamin C solution does not contain starch, it doesn't show a color change.

Standardizing the Reaction

Iodine reacts with both starch and vitamin C, even though it shows a color change only with starch. But when both starch and vitamin C are present, iodine reacts first with the vitamin C. Only when all the vitamin C is "used up" in reacting with iodine does iodine begin to react with starch and produce the color change you just observed. In this part of the activity, you will analyze a solution using a process called titration to determine how much iodine it takes to react with (or use up) 50 mg of vitamin C.

❶ Add 2.5 mL of the 1% starch solution to 50 mL of vitamin C standard solution in a beaker. Mix. The vitamin C solution has a concentration of 1 mg per mL, so we know that the 50 mL of solution contains 50 mg of vitamin C.

❷ Fill a 10-mL graduated cylinder with iodine to exactly the 10 mL mark. Take iodine from this cylinder and add it, drop by drop, to the vitamin C/starch solution you made in the previous step. Swirl the contents after each drop is added.

❸ Continue adding iodine to the vitamin C/starch solution until a blue-black color persists for at least 1 minute after swirling. When the color lasts, the endpoint of the reaction has been reached. At this stage, all of the vitamin C has reacted with the iodine, and the starch is free to react, giving a blue-black color to the solution.

❹ Determine the volume of iodine you used to reach the endpoint. Do this by putting back into the cylinder any iodine left in the dropper, and then subtracting the volume of iodine left in the graduated cylinder from 10 mL. The difference is the volume of iodine needed to react with 50 mg of vitamin C. Record this number; you'll need it later.

Steps 2, 3, and 4 are steps in titration. Now that you know how much iodine it takes to react with 50 mg of vitamin C, you can use this information to calculate the amount of vitamin C in an "unknown" sample!

Determining the Amount of Vitamin C in a Beverage

❶ Put 50 mL of the "unknown" sample you'll be testing (actually a common beverage) into a 100-mL beaker or flask. Add 2.5 mL of the 1% soluble starch solution. We will call this your unknown/starch solution.

Note: If your unknown is highly colored (like orange juice), the procedure will work best if you dilute it 1:10 first. The lighter color allows you to see the color-change reaction much more easily. If you decide to dilute, take 5 mL of the unknown and add it to 45 mL water. Ask for help in this step if needed. You will compensate for the dilution later in the activity by multiplying by 10.

❷ Titrate the unknown/starch solution with iodine, exactly as you did in steps 2 through 4. Record the volume of iodine required to reach the endpoint (the blue-black color that persists for 1 minute).

The volume of iodine in mL it took to react with 50 mg of vitamin C is proportional to the volume of iodine you just used to react with the unknown amount of vitamin C:

$$\frac{\text{mL iodine needed to react with 50 mg vit C}}{50 \text{ mg vit C}} = \frac{\text{mL iodine added to unknown}}{x \text{ mg vit C in unknown}}$$

This equation can be expressed in a way that makes it easy to solve for x, the milligrams of vitamin C in the unknown:

$$x \text{ mg vit C in unknown} = \frac{50 \text{ mg vit C} \times \text{mL of iodine added to unknown}}{\text{mL of iodine needed to react with 50 mg vit C}}$$

❸ Calculate the amount of vitamin C present in the unknown solution by using the equation above. Record the amount. If you diluted your unknown, multiply your answer by 10.

Now you can calculate the amount of vitamin C per serving in your unknown, and the percentage of the Recommended Daily Allowance (RDA) of vitamin C that it contains.

❹ First calculate how many milligrams of vitamin C are in each milliliter of the unknown. Simply divide the number of milligrams of vitamin C in the unknown by 50, which is the number of milliliters of unknown. The answer is in units of mg/mL. Record this figure.

❺ Find and record the volume of 1 serving of your unknown (this volume is listed on the nutritional label of the beverage container).

❻ Convert the volume of 1 serving from fluid ounces to milliliters. Use this conversion equivalent: 1 oz = 30 mL. Record the converted volume.

❼ Calculate the amount (mg) of vitamin C in 1 serving of the unknown. Do this by multiplying the milligrams of vitamin C per milliliter by the number of milliliters in 1 serving. Record this figure.

❽ Calculate what percentage of the RDA for vitamin C is present in 1 serving of the unknown. Do this by dividing the milligrams of vitamin C per serving by 60 mg, which is the RDA of vitamin C for adults, and then multiplying by 100 (to get a percentage). Record this percentage.

❾ If time permits, choose another "unknown" and determine the amount of vitamin C it contains.

Analyzing Data and Drawing Conclusions

How do your results compare with the information listed on the product labels for the amount of vitamin C in 1 serving? How do they compare with the RDA of vitamin C in 1 serving listed on the labels? How much of each beverage would you have to drink to receive your RDA for vitamin C?

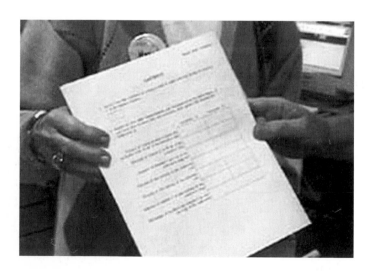

An Example

Nina and Edith found that it took 3 mL of iodine to react with 50 mg of vitamin C, and 5 mL of iodine to reach the endpoint with their unknown. Here are their calculations:

x mg vit C in unknown =

$$\frac{50 \text{ mg vit C} \times \text{mL of iodine added to unknown}}{\text{mL of iodine needed to react with 50 mg vit C}}$$

They calculated that there was 83.33 mg of vitamin C in their 50 mL of unknown:

$$\frac{50 \text{ mg} \times 5 \text{ mL}}{3 \text{ mL}} = 83.33 \text{ mg}$$

From this number they figured that there was 1.67 mg/mL of vitamin C in their unknown:

$$\frac{83.33 \text{ mg}}{50 \text{ mL}} = 1.67 \text{ mg/mL}$$

They found that a serving of their unknown was 8 oz, which they converted to mL:

$$\frac{30 \text{ mL}}{1 \text{ oz}} \times 8 \text{ oz} = 240 \text{ mL/serving}$$

They used this number to find the milligrams of vitamin C in 1 serving of the unknown:

1.67 mg/mL × 240 mL/serving = 400.8 mg vitamin C per serving

Finally, they found the percentage of the RDA for vitamin C that 400.8 mg of vitamin C is equal to:

$$\frac{400.8 \text{ mg}}{60 \text{ mg}} \times 100 = 667\%$$

Facilitator's Guide

How Much Do You C?

Materials

for the whole group

▲ vitamin C standard solution, 1 mg/mL (see Preparation)

▲ 1% starch solution (see Preparation)

▲ selection of beverages to test for vitamin C content, such as orange juice, grapefruit juice, sports drinks, apple juice drinks, etc.

for each small group

▲ about 75 mL vitamin C solution

▲ about 25 mL 1% starch solution

▲ 1 10-mL graduated cylinder

▲ 1 50- or 100-mL graduated cylinder

▲ 1 100-mL or larger beaker or flask

▲ pipette or dropper calibrated to 1 mL

▲ 2 medicine droppers

▲ potato slice or bread slice

▲ water

▲ tincture of iodine, 2% USP, 30 mL bottle

▲ access to drinks for testing

▲ paper for data collection

Management

▲ Amount of time for the activity: 45 minutes

▲ Preparation time: 30 minutes

▲ Group size: 2, 3, or 4

Preparation and Setup

Activity Overview

Determine the vitamin C content of various drinks through simple chemical titration and mathematical calculations, and then use this information to calculate the percentage of the Recommended Daily Allowance (RDA) of vitamin C that a serving of each drink contains.

Concepts

❯ Vitamin C plays an essential role in keeping humans healthy.

❯ Humans must ingest vitamin C because our bodies don't synthesize it.

❯ Food and drinks differ in the amounts of vitamin C they contain.

Preparation

❶ Obtain a selection of beverages to test for vitamin C content. Cover the parts of the nutritional labels of the beverages that show vitamin C content, but keep serving size visible.

❷ Prepare the 1 mg/mL vitamin C standard solution: Dissolve 100-mg vitamin C tablets in water at the ratio of 1 tablet for each 100 mL of water. For fifteen small groups you will need about 1200 mL of solution (75+ mL per group). The residue you may see is from inert elements in the tablets and may be ignored. Make just prior to use or refrigerate overnight.

❸ Prepare the 1% starch solution: Dissolve soluble starch (corn, potato, or rice) in water at the ratio of 1 g of starch for each 100 mL water. Gentle heating helps facilitate the process. For fifteen groups you will need about 400 mL.

❹ Obtain the other materials. Tincture of iodine is available at drugstores.

> **TIPS!**
>
> ● Encourage the dilution of strongly colored unknown samples. The color of a beverage can make it impossible to detect an accurate endpoint in the titration. Dilute 1:10; see **Note** on page 31.
>
> ● The activity can be simplified by dispensing with the calculations of vitamin C content per serving and percentage RDA.

Questions for Getting Started

❯ How many different vitamins can you name? Why are vitamins important for our bodies?

❯ What does vitamin C do in your body?

❯ What foods and drinks contain vitamin C? Is there anything about the appearance of a beverage product that suggests it contains vitamin C?

After the Exploration

Expected Results

If the assay is conducted properly and all the reagents are freshly and accurately prepared, it should take between 3 and 4 mL of iodine to reach the endpoint for the vitamin C standard titration.

It is not very difficult to obtain an accurate picture of the relative amounts of vitamin C in various beverages (i.e., drinks that contain 200% of the RDA of vitamin C will be found to consume twice as much iodine in the reaction as drinks that contain only 100% the RDA). In many cases, the absolute amounts of vitamin C calculated in the activity will be very close to those stated on the labels.

What's Going On?

The assay is based on the ability of iodine to bind more tightly to vitamin C than to starch, and the fact that the vitamin C–iodine complex is colorless but the starch/iodine complex is blue-black.

The starch added to the unknown sample serves as an indicator. When iodine is added to the unknown/starch mixture, the iodine complexes first with the vitamin C present in the unknown. Only after all the vitamin C is bound to iodine is the iodine free to react with the starch and produce the characteristic blue-black color of the starch/iodine complex.

The amount of iodine it takes to reach this endpoint can be used to calculate the amount of vitamin C present in the unknown, because the ratio of these two numbers is proportional to the ratio of iodine and vitamin C in the standard titration.

Discussion Questions

❶ Why does the blue-black color take longer to disappear from the vitamin C/starch solution the closer you get to the endpoint?

❷ What does "Recommended Daily Allowance" mean?

❸ Have you heard about people taking vitamin C to help prevent colds? Do you think this works? Do you know about any scientific research on this topic?

Going Further: Ideas for Inquiry

❯ Carry out the vitamin C assay using whole fruit: Weigh a section of orange, squeeze out the juice, and proceed as described previously. From the results you can determine the approximate mass of an orange that will yield sufficient juice to provide the RDA of vitamin C.

❯ Find out if cooking affects the vitamin C content of foods. Weigh a piece of potato, add water, and puree it in a blender. Perform the vitamin C analysis and determine the potato's vitamin C content per unit of mass. Then boil or microwave a potato, repeat the analysis, and compare the results with those for the uncooked potato.

❯ Investigate the effects of antacids on the vitamin C content of various beverages.

The Basics and Beyond

Background

Vitamin C (L-ascorbic acid) is a water-soluble vitamin found in fruits and vegetables. Humans are one of the few animals whose cells do not synthesize their own vitamin C, so we rely on taking it in through our food or from vitamin supplements.

Vitamin C plays an integral role in the synthesis of the protein collagen, which is the basis of connective tissue, the most abundant tissue in the body. Collagen binds muscle cells together, gives support and maintains shape in intervertebral discs, and allows movement in joints. It is found in fat tissue, bones, teeth, tendons, skin, and scar tissue, and is the supporting material in capillaries. Additionally, vitamin C plays an important role as an antioxidant, protecting the body's fluids from damage by free radicals generated during metabolism. This antioxidant property helps to prevent chromosome damage. Vitamin C also plays a role in amino acid metabolism and hormone synthesis.

We absorb about 80% to 90% of the vitamin C we ingest. The Recommended Daily Allowances for vitamin C are as follows:

Age (years)	0–0.5	0.5–1	1–3	4–10	11–14	15+
mg vitamin C	30	35	40	45	50	60

Beverages vary greatly in their vitamin C content. Perhaps surprisingly, many "sports drinks," which are usually colored orange or green, do not contain vitamin C. The orange or green color implies the presence of vitamin C, but these drinks state explicitly on their labels that they are not a source of vitamin C.

The table below shows an example of a set of results for a particular brand of orange juice.

	Unknown A
Volume of iodine needed to reach the endpoint with 50 mL of the unknown	5 mL
Amount of vitamin C in 50 mL of the unknown	83.33 mg
Amount of vitamin C in 1 mL of the unknown	1.67 mg/mL
Volume of 1 serving of the unknown (oz)	8 oz
Volume of 1 serving of the unknown (mL)	240 mL
Amount of vitamin C in 1 serving of the unknown	400.8 mg
Percentage of the RDA for vitamin C in 1 serving of the unknown	667%

Tidbits

❯ Scurvy is the classic symptom of vitamin C deficiency. It is characterized by hemorrhages, anemia, joint tenderness and swelling, poor wound healing, weakness, defects in skeletal calcification, hemorrhaging of the gums, loss of teeth, gingivitis, and ulceration of the mouth. Most of these symptoms are due to the improper formation of collagen. Although severe symptoms of scurvy are rarely seen in modern societies, some members of at-risk groups (such as hospitalized patients, seniors, and people on restricted diets) show mild symptoms of scurvy, including delayed wound healing and reduced resistance to infection. In adults, about 10 mg per day of vitamin C is sufficient to prevent scurvy.

❯ Vitamin C is a coenzyme for proline hydroxylase and lysyl oxidase. These enzymes convert the amino acids proline and lysine into hydroxyproline and hydroxylysine, respectively. These two amino acids are present in large amounts in collagen. When an inadequate amount of vitamin C is present, these amino acids are not produced, and their absence affects collagen structure at the tertiary level: amino acid side chains are not able to react with each other to form an elaborate three-dimensional protein structure.

❯ Vitamin C is very labile; it leaches into the cooking water of boiled foods and is rapidly oxidized when cells are exposed to the air (as when food is cut or torn). Heating and high pH also rapidly degrade vitamin C. For all of these reasons, food preparation often destroys much of the vitamin C content of food.

❯ Daily requirements for vitamin C increase with pregnancy (an additional 20 mg needed), lactation (an additional 40 mg needed), and for cigarette smokers (100 mg total recommended). Diarrhea, rheumatic fever, rheumatoid arthritis, infections, trauma, and surgery all increase the need for vitamin C as well.

Explorer's Guide

How Sweet It Is

All sugars are not created equal

Is the sugar in a candy bar any different from the sugar in a fresh piece of fruit? Find out about the different types of sugars and which ones have to be processed by our bodies before our fuel gauges are on "full" again.

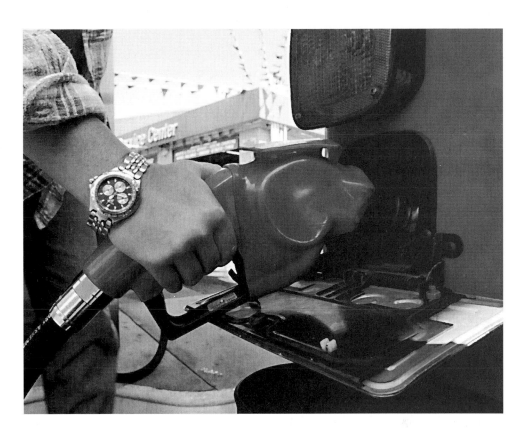

Things You Will Need

- ▲ 5 mL yeast extract
- ▲ 25 mL 5% sucrose solution
- ▲ 15 mL 5% glucose solution
- ▲ 50 mL Benedict's solution
- ▲ 20 mL water
- ▲ access to warm water
- ▲ access to a boiling water bath
- ▲ 8 test tubes
- ▲ test tube rack (for 8 tubes)
- ▲ access to a test tube holder or pot holder
- ▲ stoppers, parafilm, or plastic wrap to cover test tubes
- ▲ scissors to cut tape labels
- ▲ tape and marking pen for labels
- ▲ 1 10-mL graduated cylinder or 5 calibrated disposable pipettes
- ▲ 4 medicine droppers
- ▲ 1 large foam cup for warm water bath
- ▲ thermometer
- ▲ paper for recording observations

To Do and Notice

❶ Prepare a warm water bath at 30°–35°C in the foam cup. Place a thermometer in the cup.

❷ Use the tape and marker to label four test tubes in a rack 1A, 1B, 1C, and 1D.

❸ Add solutions to the tubes (as described at right), being sure to use a clean pipette for each different solution (if you are using a graduated cylinder, rinse it between each use).

Record the contents of each tube on a sheet of paper.

❹ Stopper or cover each tube and invert it several times to mix the contents thoroughly.

❺ Place the tubes in the warm water bath to incubate for 35 minutes. Check the temperature periodically and adjust it so that it remains between 30°C and 35°C.

❻ While your tubes are incubating, label four more test tubes 2A, 2B, 2C, and 2D. Add 10 mL of Benedict's solution to each tube.

❼ When the incubation period is complete, remove the test tubes from the water bath. This is a good stopping place for the day unless more than 60 minutes are available. Cover all of the test tubes. Refrigerate tubes 1A, 1B, 1C, and 1D overnight.

❽ When you resume, mix the contents of each of the tubes 1A, 1B, 1C, and 1D by inverting them. Remove the stoppers or covers. Using a clean dropper each time, add 16 drops of solution from each of these tubes to one of the tubes in the second set, as shown at right.

❾ Cover or stopper each of the tubes in the second set, then mix each one by inverting it.

❿ Place tubes 2A, 2B, 2C, and 2D into a boiling water bath. Leave them there for 4 minutes (it's all right if the water isn't actually boiling, but it should be very hot). After 4 minutes, remove the tubes using a test tube holder or pot holder.

⓫ Observe the contents of each test tube. If the contents of a tube remain the blue color of the Benedict's solution, the reaction is negative, which means there is no chemical change; if the contents change color to green, or if bright orange precipitate forms in the test tube, the reaction is positive.

⓬ Record the contents and the final color for each of the tubes. The record of your observations will help you interpret your results.

Analyzing Data and Drawing Conclusions

Based on your observations, what do you think has occurred in each test tube? What gives a positive reaction with Benedict's solution? Does Benedict's solution react with sucrose? Does it react with yeast extract? What does the yeast extract seem to be doing to the sucrose?

Step 3

Tube 1A:
10 mL 5% sucrose solution
+ 2 mL water

Tube 1B:
10 mL 5% sucrose solution
+ 2 mL yeast extract

Tube 1C:
10 mL 5% glucose solution
+ 2 mL water

Tube 1D:
10 mL water
+ 2 mL yeast extract

Step 8

Tube 2A:
16 drops from tube 1A

Tube 2B:
16 drops from tube 1B

Tube 2C:
16 drops from tube 1C

Tube 2D:
16 drops from tube 1D

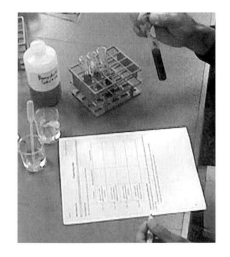

Facilitator's Guide

How Sweet It Is

Materials

for the whole group

▲ 7 oz package of dry yeast
▲ funnel
▲ coffee filter
▲ 5% glucose solution
▲ 5% sucrose solution
▲ Benedict's qualitative solution (purchased from supply house or made according to recipe in Preparation)
▲ a boiling water bath

for each pair or small group

▲ 5 mL yeast extract
▲ 25 mL 5% sucrose solution
▲ 15 mL 5% glucose solution
▲ 50 mL Benedict's solution
▲ 20 mL water
▲ access to warm water (35–40°C)
▲ access to a boiling water bath
▲ 8 test tubes
▲ test tube rack (for 8 tubes)
▲ stoppers, parafilm, or plastic wrap to cover tubes
▲ scissors to cut tape labels
▲ tape and marking pen for labels
▲ 1 10-mL graduated cylinder or 5 calibrated disposable pipettes
▲ 4 medicine droppers
▲ 1 large foam cup for warm water bath
▲ thermometer
▲ paper for recording observations

Management

▲ Amount of time for the activity: about 60 minutes total*
▲ Preparation time: 45 minutes to make all reagents
▲ Group size: 2, 3, or 4

Preparation and Setup

Activity Overview

Explore the biochemistry of sugars. Simulate how complex sugars are broken down into simple sugars by our bodies before the energy contained in the complex sugars can be utilized in cellular respiration.

Concepts

❯ Some sugars are made up of a single sugar unit and others—complex sugars—are made up of two sugar units.

❯ Complex sugars must be broken down into simple sugars for their energy to be utilized by the body.

❯ Most of the sugars in the human diet are complex sugars.

Preparation

❶ Obtain the necessary materials. Benedict's solution can be purchased from a biological supply house, or prepared as directed in step 4.

❷ Prepare yeast extract: The night before the activity, dissolve 1 package dry yeast (7 oz) in 80 mL lukewarm water. Let sit at room temperature for 20 minutes. Filter the mixture through a funnel lined with filter paper. (This takes about 1 hour; you may also perform the filtration in the refrigerator overnight.) Refrigerate the extract overnight. You will have about 50 mL of filtrate, which is sufficient for 10 groups to conduct the basic activity.

❸ Prepare the sugar solutions: At the beginning of the day, add 15 g sucrose (table sugar) to 300 mL water, and add 10 g glucose (dextrose) to 200 mL water. These 5% solutions are sufficient for 10 groups to conduct the basic activity. Keep them refrigerated during the day.

Tips!

● To simplify the activity, the fluids can be tested with glucose test strips instead of Benedict's solution, but the test strips will not detect the presence of monosaccharides other than glucose, and the results will not be as directly apparent.

● The activity "Milk Makes Me Sick" on page 43 is also about sugars.

---

*If there is insufficient time to complete the activity in one session, work can be halted after the incubation period (at which point the test tubes are put in a refrigerator) and resumed the next day.

❹ Prepare Benedict's solution (if not purchased). Obtain the following:

- 173 g sodium or potassium citrate
- 100 g anhydrous sodium carbonate
- 17.3 g crystalline copper sulfate
- distilled water

Dissolve the sodium carbonate and the citrate in 800 mL water (warm slightly to speed the process). Filter. Dissolve the copper sulfate in 100 mL water and slowly pour into the first solution. Stir constantly, let cool, and add distilled water to make 1 liter final volume. One liter will provide sufficient solution for 20 groups to conduct the basic activity.

❺ Prepare a boiling water bath before explorers reach step 10 in the investigation.

Questions for Getting Started

❯ Is sugar important to our bodies? How does the body use sugar?

❯ What is sugar? How many types of sugars are there? Can you name some different types of sugars? In what kind of food might you find each type of sugar?

After the Exploration

Expected Results

Both yeast extract alone and sucrose alone will yield negative reactions (the contents of the tubes remain the blue color of the Benedict's solution). Both glucose and sucrose with yeast extract will yield positive reactions—copious amounts of orange precipitate. The Benedict's reaction is semiquantitative; a change from blue to green indicates the presence of a small amount of simple sugar, and the formation of the orange precipitate indicates that a large amount of simple sugar is present.

Explorers should be able to conclude that glucose is the only substance that can give a positive reaction with the Benedict's solution, and that the yeast extract somehow changes the sucrose into glucose.

What's Going On?

Benedict's solution reacts with a free carbonyl group (a carbon double-bonded to an oxygen). Monosaccharides have a free carbonyl group, but disaccharides do not, because the carbonyl group is the site at which the bonding of the monosaccharide units occurs. Therefore, Benedict's solution cannot react with sugars that are not monosaccharides.

Glucose serves as a positive control for the Benedict's solution; it is a monosaccharide and will give a positive reaction. The water and yeast extract serve as a negative control, showing that the yeast extract does not contain glucose. The sucrose and yeast extract together give a positive reaction because the yeast extract contains the enzyme invertase, which breaks down sucrose into its component simple sugars, glucose and fructose. The enzyme is called invertase because it breaks down the sucrose to an "invert" sugar—one that is half glucose and half fructose.

The invertase enzyme is produced by active yeast because yeasts are in the same boat as humans: they cannot metabolize sucrose directly, but must first break the disaccharide down into its monosaccharide components. The period of incubation in the warm water bath mimics the conditions in which human enzymes in the small intestine break disaccharides down into simple sugars.

Discussion Questions

❶ Why was a tube of yeast and water included in the experiment? If it was omitted, would that affect your ability to draw conclusions?

❷ What percentage of your diet do you think consists of carbohydrates (sugars and starches)?

❸ Why are certain food products advertised as "sugar-free"? What gives these sugar-free products their sweet flavor? Do you have any health concerns about consuming artificially sweetened foods?

Going Further: Ideas for Inquiry

❯ Form hypotheses about the presence of glucose in familiar foods and drinks, and then test for glucose with Benedict's solution. When the result is negative, see if a yeast extract will break down the sugars or starches to monosaccharides.

❯ Track the time course of the invertase reaction. After the sucrose is mixed with the yeast extract and incubated, remove samples and test them with Benedict's solution at 5-minute intervals.

❯ Explore the effects of temperature on the ability of the yeast extract to degrade complex sugars.

❯ List what you eat during a typical day or series of days and use this information to estimate the percentage of your diet made up of carbohydrates.

The Basics and Beyond

Background

Sugars are a type of carbohydrate made up of carbon, hydrogen, and oxygen. Atoms of these elements are always present in a ratio of 1:2:1; the chemical formula for glucose, for example, is $C_6H_{12}O_6$. Some sugars, such as glucose, fructose, and galactose, consist of a single sugar unit and are called simple sugars or monosaccharides. Other sugars are formed from the bonding of two monosaccharides; these complex sugars, called disaccharides, include common table sugar, or sucrose. A sucrose molecule is made up of a molecule of glucose and a molecule of fructose bonded together.

Disaccharides—mostly sucrose and the milk sugar, lactose—make up the bulk of the sugar in the human diet. These complex sugars are an important source of energy, but before our bodies can utilize the energy stored in them, they must be broken down into their monosaccharide components (see Figure 1). This process is accomplished by enzymes in the small intestine called saccharidases. Through their action, all the complex sugars we ingest are broken down into three simple sugars: glucose, galactose, and fructose. These simple sugars are then absorbed across the intestinal mucosa and transported via the portal vein to the liver. In the liver, galactose and fructose are enzymatically converted to glucose. The only sugar normally found in the blood is glucose. Glucose is the primary fuel for the process of cellular respiration, which is what provides our cells with energy.

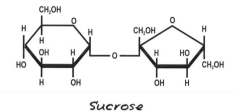

Figure 1: Sucrose and its breakdown products, glucose and fructose

Tidbits

❯ In Western societies, about half the body's caloric needs are derived from carbohydrates (sugars and starches). In Eastern and developing countries, carbohydrates are the major source of calories in the diet.

❯ Glucose can be stored in liver and muscle cells in the form of a polymer called glycogen. In glycogen, the glucose units are bound together in branching structures. When blood glucose levels are low, the liver can release glucose into the blood. When blood glucose levels are high, the excess can be stored as glycogen.

Explorer's Guide
Milk Makes Me Sick!

Find out why many people can't drink milk

Is milk really good for everybody? Fact is, flatulence and stomach cramps are the reward for most people worldwide if they do drink milk, but sometimes they can do something to prevent getting sick.

Things You Will Need

- ▲ beaker of "milk A"
- ▲ beaker of "milk B"
- ▲ access to a bottle of "mystery drops"
- ▲ beaker of 2% glucose solution
- ▲ beaker of water
- ▲ glucose test strips and color key
- ▲ dilution tray with 4 wells, or 4 small test tubes
- ▲ 2 medicine droppers
- ▲ toothpicks
- ▲ tape and pen for labeling
- ▲ stopwatch or watch with second hand
- ▲ paper for recording data

To Do and Notice

This activity works best with a facilitator.

Milk A is regular nonfat milk, the kind that many people have trouble digesting. Milk B is specially treated milk that can be digested by just about everybody. You will be testing both milk samples to figure out why one gives some people digestive troubles and the other does not.

❶ Examine milk A and milk B. Observe their similarities and differences. Use as many of your senses as possible (but don't taste!). Record your observations.

By using observation alone, you will not be able to notice an important chemical difference in the two kinds of milk: the amount of the sugar glucose they each contain. You will use the glucose test strips to measure this difference.

❷ The test strips must be used *exactly* as directed on the package. Read the package information.

❸ First, you need to find out how the glucose test strips respond to a solution with a known concentration of glucose and to plain water (no glucose at all). Dip a strip into the 2% glucose solution and compare its color to the color key. Does the color of the strip match the color for 2% glucose? Is it higher or lower? Record the result. Now dip a fresh test strip into the plain water and compare its color to the color key. Record the result.

❹ Use tape and a pen to label one medicine dropper "A" and the other "B." Use dropper A with milk A only, and use dropper B with milk B only.

❺ Label 2 wells of a dilution tray (or two test tubes) "A1" and "B1." Add 20 drops of milk A into well A1, and 20 drops of milk B into well B1.

❻ Use a glucose test strip to determine the glucose concentration of the sample of milk A. Record the glucose concentration.

❼ Use a fresh glucose test strip to determine the concentration of glucose in the sample of milk B. Record its glucose concentration also.

❽ Label 2 clean wells or test tubes "A2" and "B2." Add 20 drops of milk A to well A2, and 20 drops of milk B to well B2.

❾ Add 1 drop of "mystery drops" to the milk in well A2. Mix with a toothpick and let it sit for 1 minute.

❿ Test the glucose concentration of the sample of milk A in well A2 with a fresh test strip. Record the result.

⓫ Add 1 drop of "mystery drops" to the milk in well B2. Mix with a fresh toothpick and let it sit for 1 minute.

⓬ Test the glucose concentration of the sample of milk B in well B2 with a fresh test strip. Record the result.

Analyzing Data and Drawing Conclusions

What can you conclude about the amount of glucose contained in milk A as compared to milk B? Was there a change in milk A after you added the mystery drops? If so, what was it? Is it possible that the mystery drops themselves contain glucose? Where does the glucose come from? How can you rule out this possibility? What can you conclude about milk A?

Facilitator's Guide
Milk Makes Me Sick!

Materials

for the whole group

▲ nonfat milk ("milk A")

▲ lactose-free milk (e.g., Lactaid) ("milk B")

▲ 1 or more bottles of lactase drops (e.g., Dairy Ease), with label covered ("mystery drops")

▲ 2% glucose solution

for each small group

▲ 20 mL milk A

▲ 20 mL milk B

▲ 10 mL of 2% glucose solution

▲ access to mystery drops

▲ water

▲ dilution tray (4 wells, 3 mL each) or 4 small test tubes

▲ 4 beakers or clear cups for holding milks, water, glucose

▲ 2 medicine droppers

▲ 8 glucose test strips for testing urine and color key

▲ toothpicks

▲ tape and pen for labeling

▲ stopwatch or watch with second hand

▲ paper for recording data

Management

▲ Amount of time for the activity: 30–45 minutes

▲ Preparation time: 40 minutes

▲ Group size: 2, 3, or 4

| Preparation and Setup

Activity Overview

Learn the biochemical basis of lactose intolerance by testing for the presence of glucose in regular milk and in milk to which the enzyme lactase has been added.

Concepts

❯ Milk contains the sugar lactose.

❯ Lactase is an enzyme that breaks down lactose into glucose and galactose.

❯ Some people's bodies cannot produce lactase; when they consume dairy products, they may have digestive trouble.

❯ Enzymes speed up chemical reactions.

Preparation

❶ Prepare the 2% glucose solution by dissolving glucose in water to a final concentration of 2 g of glucose for each 100 mL of water. Glucose tablets may be purchased at drugstores. Make sure the package is labeled with the amount of glucose in each tablet.

❷ Obtain the glucose test strips, which are sold in drugstores for testing urine. They may be cut in half lengthwise to double the quantity.

❸ Cover the label of the bottle containing the lactase.

Questions for Getting Started

❯ Have you heard of enzymes before? Can you give some examples?

❯ What do enzymes do in your body?

| After the Exploration

Expected Results

No glucose should be detected in regular milk (milk A), but a significant amount should be found in the specially treated milk (milk B). After the mystery drops are added, both milk samples should be found to contain glucose.

Explorers should be able to deduce from their results that the addition of the mystery drops leads to the presence of glucose in milk A. An important part of this process is testing the mystery drops themselves for the presence of glucose, to eliminate the possibility that the drops are simply adding glucose to the regular milk.

Once explorers have concluded that the mystery drops change a substance in the milk into glucose, they may be able to reason that the substance in milk A that the mystery drops change into glucose is the substance some people cannot digest.

When investigators have reached this conclusion, the facilitator can reveal the rest of the story: the problem substance is the sugar lactose; the mystery drops are the enzyme lactase, which breaks down lactose into glucose and another simple sugar; people who can't digest milk aren't able to produce lactase in their bodies.

What's Going On?

Regular milk contains a high concentration of lactose and no glucose. The lactose-free milk, however, has been treated with lactase, the enzyme that breaks down lactose into glucose and galactose. Because of this treatment, the lactose-free milk will show the presence of glucose.

When lactase drops are added to the regular milk, its lactose is broken down into glucose and galactose, and it becomes just like the lactose-free milk. Adding lactase to the lactose-free milk causes no changes because the milk lacks any lactose for the lactase to act on.

Discussion Questions

❶ Are you lactose intolerant? Do you know other people who are lactose intolerant?

❷ What happens when lactose-intolerant people eat dairy products?

Going Further: Ideas for Inquiry

❯ Test fermented dairy products such as yogurt and kefir for the presence of glucose in order to make inferences about how much lactose they contain. Find out how the process of fermentation may account for your results.

❯ Test different types of milk, such as goat milk and soy "milk," for the presence of glucose.

❯ Nearly all enzymes are proteins, and their ability to function is based on their three-dimensional structure. Therefore, any conditions that affect protein structure may also affect enzyme function. These conditions include heat, extremes of pH, and salinity. Test the effects of these factors on lactase function by treating lactase in a variety of ways (heating it to boiling, adding salt, adding acid) and then testing its ability to convert the lactose in regular milk into glucose and galactose. Compare these results to those obtained using untreated lactase.

❯ Enzymes speed up chemical reactions. Explore the effects of temperature on lactose enzyme activity.

The Basics and Beyond

Background

Milk contains the sugar lactose. A lactose molecule is made up of two parts: the simple sugars glucose and galactose. For lactose to be digested and its energy absorbed by the body, it must be broken down into these constituent parts. This job is performed in the human body by the enzyme lactase.

Although most young children have the ability to produce lactase, many adults do not. The gene that codes for production of the enzyme has been "turned off." These people are said to be lactose intolerant. When they ingest dairy products, they experience uncomfortable symptoms such as diarrhea, excess gas, and stomach cramps.

These symptoms occur because the lactose is not digested. The relatively large lactose molecules accumulate in the large intestine and affect the osmotic balance there. They cause water to enter the intestine, resulting in watery stool or diarrhea. In addition, the lactose is fermented by the friendly bacteria that normally inhabit the large intestine, producing organic acids and intestinal gas.

Most people who are lactose intolerant choose to avoid lactose-containing milk products. They can also use special dairy products in which the lactose has already been broken down. One of these types of products, lactose-free milk, is used in this activity.

Tidbits

❯ Most humans all over the world are born with the gene that codes for production of lactase, and as infants produce ample quantities of lactase for milk digestion. As many humans mature, however, they completely or partially lose the ability to produce lactase because of changes in the lactase gene. Some people experience a gradual decline in lactase

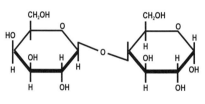

Lactose

Galactose + Glucose

Figure 1: Lactose molecule converted to galactose and glucose

production throughout their lives; others lose the ability to produce lactase more suddenly at some time after childhood.

❯ The ability to digest lactose as an adult appears to be genetically determined. There is a strong correlation between being able to digest lactose as an adult and being descended from an ethnic group that practiced dairying as a means of subsistence. For example, 91.5% of northern Europeans and 91.3% of the Tussi in Africa can digest lactose as adults, and both groups have relied heavily on dairying. In contrast, only 15.5% of the nondairying Yoruba and Hausa peoples of Africa are able to digest lactose, and the percentage of lactose-tolerant people in some ethnic groups is even lower.

❯ In the vast majority of ethnic groups worldwide, the adults are mostly lactose intolerant. All Eskimos and American Indians studied thus far, as well as most sub-Saharan African, Mediterranean, Near Eastern, Indian, Southeast and East Asian, and Pacific peoples, are lactose intolerant as adults.

❯ Anthropologists speculate that early in human evolution, the normal condition was for the lactase gene to be "turned off" after childhood. Later, in some groups that began to domesticate animals, the ability to digest the animals' milk provided a survival advantage. For example, in those groups located in cold climates where people could not grow crops year round, the ability to digest milk products without becoming seriously ill would confer a survival advantage, and that genetic tendency would be passed on to the next generation.

Additional Resource

"Cultural Mediation: The Evolution of Adult Lactose Absorption" in *Coevolution; Genes, Culture and Human Diversity* by William H. Durham. Stanford, Calif.: Stanford University Press, 1991.

Explorer's Guide

Got Blood?

*There's A, B, AB, and O.
How can you tell which
is which?*

Would you like to save
someone's life some day by
donating some of your blood?
If you donate blood, a test
will be done to determine what
"type" it is. Find out what
blood typing is all about.

Things You Will Need

▲ 3-oz paper cups
▲ 8 toothpicks
▲ marker for labeling cups

▲ 4 blood-typing stations
with simulated blood and
testing fluids
▲ paper for recording observations

To Do and Notice

This activity works best with a facilitator.

There are four blood-typing stations set up in the room. You will go
to each one and test the "blood" there with the two testing fluids
provided. You will observe the reaction of each test, and use these
observations to determine the blood type at each station. Leave all of
the materials at each station.

❶ At your first station, place 3 mL of the "blood" into a container.
Label the container with the station number and "anti-A."

❷ Add 10 drops of the anti-A testing fluid to the blood and mix with a
toothpick. This fluid simulates an anti-A antiserum. When real blood is
typed, anti-A antiserum reacts with markers called A antigens on the
surface of the red blood cells in the blood.

❸ Observe and record what happens. If the blood clumps, as shown in Figure 1A, the reaction is positive. You can record a positive reaction with a plus sign (+). If nothing happens to the blood, as shown in Figure 1B, the reaction is negative. This reaction can be recorded with a minus sign (–).

❹ Place another 3 mL of the same blood into another container. Label the container with the station number and "anti-B."

❺ Add 10 drops of the anti-B testing fluid to the blood and mix with a fresh toothpick. This fluid simulates an anti-B antiserum, which is used in blood typing to detect the presence of B antigens on the surface of the red blood cells in the blood.

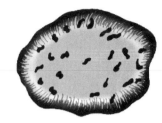

Figure 1A: Positive reaction

❻ Observe and record what happens.

❼ Repeat the procedure at each of the other three stations. Record your results each time.

Interpreting Your Observations

Use the information below to determine which blood type is being simulated at each station.

Figure 1B: Negative reaction

Table 1

Antigens on Red Blood Cells*	Blood Type
A	A
B	B
both A and B	AB
neither A nor B	O

*A positive reaction to the anti-A antiserum means the blood contains the A antigen; a positive reaction to the anti-B antiserum means the blood contains the B antigen.

Facilitator's Guide
Got Blood?

Materials

for the whole group

▲ about 250 mL of nonfat milk
▲ about 250 mL of water
▲ red and green food coloring
▲ 100 mL of white vinegar
▲ 100 mL water
▲ 12 flasks or containers to hold "blood" and "antisera"
▲ 4 droppers, with 1-mL calibrations
▲ 8 droppers (calibrations unnecessary)
▲ string to attach droppers to containers
▲ tape for labeling containers

for each pair or small group

▲ 8 3-oz paper cups
▲ 8 toothpicks
▲ marker for labeling
▲ paper for recording observations

Management

▲ Amount of time for the activity: 30 minutes
▲ Preparation time: 30–45 minutes
▲ Group size: 2, 3, or 4

Preparation and Setup

Activity Overview

Use simulated blood and antisera to model the immune responses used to determine ABO blood group.

Concepts

❯ Antigens on the surfaces of our cells help our immune systems distinguish between cells that belong in the body and cells that don't.

❯ The presence or absence of two antigens, A and B, on red blood cells determines which of the four blood groups, or types, a person's blood belongs to: A, B, AB, or O.

❯ The immune reaction of anti-A and anti-B antibodies with their antigens is used to "type" a sample of blood.

Preparation

❶ To make enough simulated blood for 15 groups: Dilute nonfat milk by one-half (i.e., 250 mL milk and 250 mL water). Mix thoroughly. Add red and green food coloring. (We recommend about 75 drops red and 5 drops green.) Refrigerate until use.

❷ Set up the blood-typing stations. Each lab station will have the same simulated "blood" but a different set of simulated antisera, as shown in Table 2 on the next page. When the antiserum is vinegar, it will produce a simulated positive reaction; when it is water, the reaction will be negative. It is critical that the antisera listed for each blood group be kept with that blood group, or the activity will not work properly. Set up the stations as far apart as possible to minimize the chances of mixing up the antisera.

Tips!

● Put the simulated antisera into small dropper bottles for easier use.

● Follow this activity with the closely related activity "Mother and Child Reunion" (page 55). Since similar materials are used in both activities, you can save time in preparation. Moreover, this activity provides excellent background for "Mother and Child Reunion." If you plan to do both activities, prepare 1100 mL of simulated blood by diluting 550 mL of milk with 550 mL of water and coloring it with 150 drops of red food coloring and 10 drops of green.

a. Put about 120 mL of simulated blood in each of four containers.

b. Put about 25 mL of vinegar in each of four containers, and 25 mL of water in another four.

c. At station 1, place a container of simulated blood labeled "1," a container of vinegar labeled "anti-A," and a container of water labeled "anti-B."

d. Set up the other three stations with the appropriately labeled blood and antisera containers, as shown in Table 2.

e. Attach calibrated droppers to the blood containers and uncalibrated droppers to the antisera containers with string and tape. Do not reveal which blood group will be simulated at each station.

Table 2

Station	Simulated Antisera	Simulated Blood Type
1	anti-A = vinegar anti-B = water	A
2	anti-A = water anti-B = vinegar	B
3	anti-A = vinegar anti-B = vinegar	AB
4	anti-A = water anti-B = water	O

Questions for Getting Started

❯ Do you know what your blood type is? Why might you need to know your blood type?

❯ What is a blood transfusion? Why might someone need to have one?

After the Exploration

Expected Results

Table 3 summarizes the results that should be obtained at each station.

Table 3

	Station 1	Station 2	Station 3	Station 4
Reaction to anti-A	+	−	+	−
Reaction to anti-B	−	+	+	−
Blood group	A	B	AB	O

What's Going On?

When the "antiserum" is vinegar, its low pH denatures (unravels the three-dimensional structure of) the proteins in the milk, causing a visible clumping. In real blood, when a positive antibody–antigen reaction occurs, antibodies bind to many of the antigens on the red blood cell surface, forming a network that looks like clumps. The antisera at each station are set up to simulate the reactions that would occur with real blood of groups A, B, AB, and O, respectively.

Discussion Questions

❶ Blood type O is called the "universal donor" and type AB is called the "universal recipient" for blood transfusions. Why do you think that this is so?

❷ How might a determination of blood type be used to solve a crime?

Going Further: Ideas for Inquiry

❯ Learn about blood banking, blood types, blood donation, and the uses of donated blood by doing some research or talking with a staff member at a local blood bank.

❯ You may have heard of blood types being called "positive" and "negative." These names have to do with the presence or absence of another type of antigen on the surface of red blood cells called the rhesus factor, or Rh factor for short. Find out more about the Rh factor and why it may cause problems during pregnancy.

The Basics and Beyond

Background

Cells in our bodies have markers called antigens on their surfaces. These antigens are part of the body's immune system, which works to recognize cells that belong in the body ("self") and cells that don't ("nonself"). When immune-system cells find a cell with antigens they don't recognize, they produce antibodies that attach to the antigens; this marks the cell for destruction by other immune-system cells.

Two different antigens that can be present on the surface of red blood cells are the basis for the ABO blood group system, or what is commonly called blood type. Some people have the A antigen on their red blood cells, some have the B antigen, some have both, and some have neither.

The plasma (liquid) portion of each person's blood contains antibodies against the antigens not present on their own red blood cells. If your red blood cells only have the A antigen, for example, then your plasma has the anti-B antibody. The table below shows which antibodies and antigens are present in each blood group.

Table 4

Group	Antigens	Antibodies
A	A	anti-B
B	B	anti-A
AB	AB	neither
O	neither	both

If the anti-B antibody comes in contact with the B antigen, or the anti-A antibody finds the A antigen, the antibodies bind to their corresponding antigens. The result is a clumping of the red blood cells. If this occurs in a person's body (when they are given the wrong kind of blood), it could be fatal.

But the clumping reaction can also be used to determine the blood group of blood drawn from a person's body. The blood is combined with a liquid called antiserum that contains anti-A antibodies. Then a second sample of the blood is combined with antiserum that contains anti-B antibodies. The resulting clumping or lack of clumping in each test allows the blood to be "typed."

Tidbits

❯ Antibodies to nonself blood types (those that are not yours) are developed during infancy. This recognition by the body of nonself entities entering the body is mediated by the immune system.

❯ The immune system will launch an attack against anything it identifies as nonself—a virus, bacterium, parasite, transfused blood, or transplanted organ. This amazing system keeps us healthy, but it also presents challenges to physicians when an organ is transplanted. Then, strong drugs that suppress the immune system are administered until the transplant is accepted by the body.

❯ Some biotechnology companies are attempting to genetically engineer pigs so that their organs express human antigens on their surfaces. The hope is that pig organ transplants may be readily accepted by the human body and that pigs might provide an unlimited source of organs for transplant.

Explorer's Guide

Mother and Child Reunion

Use genetic detective work to match three babies with their mothers

Last Friday at Oakview Hospital, Beth gave birth to fraternal (nonidentical) twins and Sarah had a single child. Soon after, a serious fire broke out in the hospital. The three babies in the nursery were rescued, but they lost their identifying bracelets. Beth and Sarah need to be certain of the identities of the babies. Your job is to help them, using your skill at blood typing and your knowledge of how blood types are inherited.

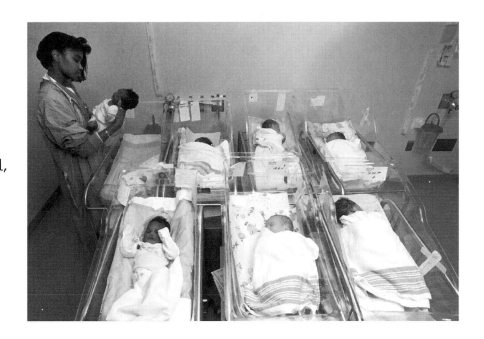

Things You Will Need

▲ 10 small paper cups
▲ 10 toothpicks
▲ marker for labeling cups

▲ 5 blood-typing stations with simulated blood and testing fluids
▲ paper for recording data

To Do and Notice

This activity works best with a facilitator.

Review the genetic basis of blood type and how the blood-type gene is inherited (see the activity "Got Blood?," page 49) before you do this activity. You will need to know about the patterns of blood-type inheritance to solve the mystery.

Samples of simulated blood from each mother and each baby have been prepared. You will test each of these samples with the two testing fluids provided, observe the reaction of each test, and use these observations to determine the blood type of each sample.

Begin at one of the five stations and then rotate through the remaining four. Leave all of the materials at each station.

❶ Get a sheet of paper on which to record your observations and conclusions. You'll find it helpful to create a data table before you begin the activity. Read through all the steps that follow, determine what kinds of data you'll be collecting, and make a data table with a place for each observation or result.

❷ At your first station, place 3 mL of the "blood" into a paper cup. Label the cup with the blood donor's name and "anti-A."

❸ Add 10 drops of anti-A testing fluid to the blood and mix with a toothpick. This fluid simulates an anti-A antiserum. When real blood is typed, anti-A antiserum detects the presence of markers called A antigens on the surface of the red blood cells in the blood.

❹ Observe what happens. If the blood clumps, the reaction is positive, which means that the A antigen is present in the blood. You can record a positive reaction with a plus sign (+). If the blood doesn't clump, the reaction is negative and the A antigen is not present. This reaction can be recorded with a minus sign (–).

❺ Place another 3 mL of the same blood into another paper cup. Label the cup with the blood donor's name and "anti-B."

❻ Add 10 drops of anti-B testing fluid to the blood and mix with a fresh toothpick. This fluid simulates an anti-B antiserum, which is used in blood typing to detect the presence of B antigens on the surface of the red blood cells in the blood.

❼ Observe the reaction and record it. This time, a positive reaction signals the presence of the B antigen.

❽ Repeat steps 2–7 at each of the other stations. Record your results each time.

Analyzing Data and Drawing Conclusions

Determine each person's blood type using the information in Table 1. Record the blood types in your data table.

When you have determined each person's blood type, use your knowledge of blood group inheritance to determine the possible blood-type genotypes of each mother and each baby.

Now use your reasoning ability to answer the following questions:

❯ Which two babies are Beth's twins?

❯ Which baby is Sarah's?

❯ Now that you know the mother of each baby, can you narrow down each baby's genotype?

❯ What blood type is the twin's father?

❯ What are the possible blood types of the father of Sarah's baby? (Explain!)

Table 1

Antigens on Red Blood Cells*	Blood Type	Genotype
A	A	AA or AO
B	B	BB or BO
both	AB	AB
neither	O	OO

*A positive reaction to the anti-A antiserum means the blood contains the A antigen; a positive reaction to the anti-B antiserum means the blood contains the B antigen.

Facilitator's Guide
Mother and Child Reunion

Materials

for the whole group

▲ about 300 mL of nonfat milk
▲ about 300 mL of water
▲ red and green food coloring
▲ 150 mL white vinegar
▲ 100 mL water
▲ 15 flasks or containers to hold "blood" and "antisera"
▲ 5 droppers with 1-mL calibrations
▲ 10 droppers (calibrations unnecessary)
▲ string to attach droppers to containers
▲ tape for labeling containers

for each small group

▲ 10 small paper cups (or similar containers)
▲ 10 toothpicks
▲ marker for labeling
▲ paper for recording data

Management

▲ Amount of time for the activity: 30 minutes
▲ Preparation time: 30–45 minutes
▲ Group size: 2–6

TIP!

● "Got Blood?" (page 49) serves as a good foundation for this activity. If you plan to do both activities, mix up an adequate amount of simulated blood when you prepare for "Got Blood?"

Preparation and Setup

Activity Overview

Use knowledge of blood groups and blood-group inheritance to solve a simulated mystery in which three babies have been separated from their birth mothers.

Concepts

❯ The gene that determines a person's blood group (commonly known as blood type) has more than two forms.

❯ Each person inherits two blood-type genes, one from the father and one from the mother.

❯ Both of the blood-type genes a person inherits are expressed; in other words, they are codominant.

Preparation

You will set up five different lab stations, each with the same simulated "blood" but a different set of simulated antisera, as shown in Table 2. When the antiserum is vinegar, it will produce a simulated positive reaction; when it is water, the reaction will be negative. It is critical that the antisera listed for each blood donor be kept with the "blood" from that donor, or the activity will not work properly; you might want to label all the materials for a station with the station number. To prevent mixups of the materials, it is helpful to spread the stations out around the room. Explorers will determine which blood group is being simulated at each station, and this information will serve as the basis for their subsequent genetic detective work.

❶ To make enough simulated blood for 15 groups: Dilute nonfat milk by one-half (i.e., 300 mL milk and 300 mL water). Mix thoroughly. Add red and green food coloring until it becomes an appropriately grotesque color. (We recommend about 75 drops red and 5 drops green.) Refrigerate until used.

❷ Put about 120 mL of simulated blood in each of five containers.

❸ Put about 25 mL of vinegar in each of six containers, and 25 mL of water in another four.

❹ At station 1, place a container of simulated blood labeled "Donor=Beth," a container of water labeled "anti-A," and a container of water labeled "anti-B."

❺ Attach a calibrated dropper to the blood container and uncalibrated droppers to the antisera containers with string and tape.

❻ Set up the other four stations with the appropriately labeled blood and antisera containers and droppers, as shown in Table 2.

Table 2

Station	Simulated Antisera	Blood Donor
1	anti-A = water anti-B = water	Beth
2	anti-A = vinegar anti-B = vinegar	Sarah
3	anti-A = vinegar anti-B = vinegar	Baby 1
4	anti-A = water anti-B = vinegar	Baby 2
5	anti-A = vinegar anti-B = water	Baby 3

Questions for Getting Started

❯ Do you know what your blood type is?

❯ If you know your blood type, can you figure out which types your mother and father could be?

After the Exploration

Expected Results

Table 3 summarizes the results that should be obtained at each station, and the conclusions that should be drawn from these results.

Table 3

	Beth	Sarah	Baby 1	Baby 2	Baby 3
Reaction to anti-A	–	+	+	–	+
Reaction to anti-B	–	+	+	+	–
Blood group (type)	0	AB	AB	B	A
Possible genotypes based on blood group	00	AB	AB	BO or BB	AO or AA
Genotypes based on known maternity	00	AB	AB	BO	AO

The following conclusions should be reached about who is related to whom:

❯ Baby 2 and Baby 3 are Beth's twins.

❯ Baby 1 is Sarah's baby.

❯ The genotype of Baby 2 must be BO; that of Baby 3 must be AO.

❯ The twins' father's blood group must be AB.

❯ The father of Sarah's baby could be blood group A, B, or AB, and could not be group O (genotypically, he must be AB, AA, BB, AO, or BO).

What's Going On?

Baby 1's only possible genotype is AB, which means that one of its parents gave it the A allele and the other gave it the B allele. Beth can therefore not be Baby 1's mother, since with blood group O she has neither the A allele nor the B allele. Since Beth is ruled out as Baby 1's mother, Sarah must be Baby 1's mother and Beth's twins must be Baby 2 and Baby 3. This conclusion is consistent with the blood groups of Beth and the two babies.

Since Baby 2 is blood group B and its mother is blood group O, it must have inherited an O allele from its mother and must therefore be genotype BO. By the same logic, Baby 3 must be genotype AO.

The father of the twins must be genotype AB because Beth couldn't have given Baby 2 its B allele or Baby 3 its A allele.

Sarah could have given either the A allele or the B allele to Baby 1, so we can't conclude which allele came from the father. We do know, however, that the father could not have contributed an O allele, which means he could not be blood group O. His genotype, therefore, could be any of the possible combinations except OO.

Discussion Questions

❶ Can blood type alone definitively identify someone's parent or child? What other genetically inherited traits could be used for such an identification?

❷ Some blood types are common in the general population, while others are rare. Why do you think this is so?

❸ If your mother's brother is blood group AB and your mother is blood group O, what are the blood groups of your maternal grandparents? Can you tell what their genotypes are? [Answer: One grandparent must have the blood group A and the genotype AO, and the other grandparent must have the blood group B and the genotype BO.]

❹ Maya is blood group A and her husband Martin is blood group B. If they have children together, what are all the possible blood groups and genotypes of these children? [Answer: The possible blood groups depend on the parents' genotypes, which we don't know. None of the blood groups can be ruled out, and the only blood group we know is possible is AB.]

Going Further: Ideas for Inquiry

❯ Find out the blood type of as many of your relatives as you can and construct a pedigree chart of the inheritance pattern in your family.

❯ Do all blood types occur with equal frequency in the population? Do they vary by race and nationality? Are some common and others rare? Do some research and find out!

The Basics and Beyond

Background

Blood type, or blood group, is determined by the presence or absence of two antigens on the surface of red blood cells. For example, blood with antigen A is type A. The other blood types are shown in Table 4.

A single gene with three different forms carries instructions for these antigens. The A form, or allele, of the gene tells cells to coat themselves with the A antigen; the B allele has instructions for the B antigen; the O allele tells cells to coat with neither antigen. Each person inherits two copies of this gene, one from the mother and one from the father. Therefore, there are six possible genotypes, or combinations, of alleles: AA, AO, BB, BO, AB, and OO. These genotypes determine a person's blood group as shown in Table 4.

Table 4

Genotype	Antigens on Red Blood Cells	Blood Group
AA or AO	A	A
BB or BO	B	B
AB	both	AB
OO	neither	O

Once a person's blood group is known, this pattern of inheritance makes it possible to reach certain conclusions about the person's blood-group genotype and the possible genotypes of the person's parents or children. For example, a person with the blood group O must have the OO genotype, and the genotype of neither parent could have been AA, BB, or AB.

Explorer's Guide

Fruitful DNA Extraction

See and touch the hereditary molecules

Do you think you have very much in common with a kiwi fruit? Believe it or not, a kiwi's genetic material is very similar to your own! See and touch the genetic material that you'll extract from the cells of a kiwi fruit.

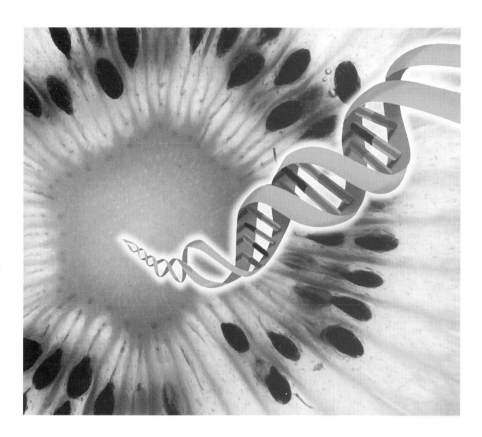

Things You Will Need

- ▲ 1 500-mL or larger beaker, or 1 250-mL or larger flask
- ▲ 2 200-mL or larger graduated beakers
- ▲ 1 100-mL graduated cylinder
- ▲ 1 100-mL beaker
- ▲ a kiwi fruit
- ▲ knife and fork for cutting and mashing
- ▲ thermometer
- ▲ funnel
- ▲ paper coffee filter to fit in the funnel
- ▲ 2 saucepans for water baths
- ▲ ice
- ▲ cold water

- ▲ hot water
- ▲ 50 mL chilled ethanol
- ▲ 2 g table salt
- ▲ 10 mL detergent
- ▲ coffee stirrers
- ▲ waxed paper or paper plate
- ▲ access to a balance
- ▲ hot plate (optional)
- ▲ clock or watch
- ▲ 1 test tube for each group member
- ▲ rack for holding test tubes
- ▲ 1 medicine dropper
- ▲ hook made from thin wire (optional)

To Do and Notice

Extracting the DNA

❶ Prepare an ice water bath by putting ice and water into a saucepan or similar container to a depth of 5 to 8 cm. Put about 50 mL of chilled ethanol into the 100-mL beaker and place the beaker in the ice bath.

❷ Prepare the DNA extraction solution: Dissolve 2 g of salt in 90 mL of water in a 200-mL or larger beaker. Then add 10 mL of detergent and stir (gently!) with a stirrer.

❸ Peel the kiwi fruit over waxed paper or a paper plate and cut it into chunks.

❹ Use a balance to measure 30 g of kiwi chunks, then thoroughly mash that amount with a fork.

❺ Place the mashed kiwi in a 200-mL or larger beaker.

❻ Pour the DNA extraction solution (detergent and salt solution from step 2) over the fruit until the total volume of fruit and liquid is about twice the volume of the mashed fruit alone.

❼ Prepare a hot water bath by putting hot water into a saucepan about 5 to 8 cm deep. Check the temperature of the hot water bath with the thermometer. Add colder or hotter water to get the water to 60°C. If you have a hot plate, put the water bath on it to help it reach and maintain a 60° temperature. Check the temperature periodically and adjust as needed.

❽ Place the beaker with fruit and extraction solution into the hot water bath. Note the time.

❾ Let the fruit and extraction solution mixture incubate in the hot water bath for 10 to 15 minutes. Stir the solution occasionally to distribute the heat. The temperature of the water bath must be monitored and maintained between 50°C and 60°C during this incubation period.

❿ After 10 or 15 minutes of incubation, transfer the beaker containing the fruit and extraction solution mixture to the ice bath. Allow it to stay there for 5 minutes, stirring occasionally as it cools.

⓫ While the extraction mixture is cooling, set up the filtration system. Place a funnel over a clean 500-mL or larger beaker or 250-mL flask, and insert a coffee filter into the funnel.

⓬ Pour the cooled extraction mixture into the filter-lined funnel. Allow the liquid to filter for about 5 minutes.

⓭ Thoroughly swirl the filtrate (the fluid that drains through the filter).

⓮ Pour about 5 mL of the filtrate into a test tube.

Precipitating the DNA

❶ Gently layer about 10 mL of cold ethanol (as cold as possible) on top of the filtrate. You can add the ethanol with a dropper or gently pour it down the side of the test tube while you hold it at an angle.

❷ Place the test tube in a test tube rack. Observe what's happening in the test tube at the area where the ethanol and filtrate layers meet. Record your observations.

❸ Let the solution sit for 2 minutes without disturbing it. A white precipitate will form in the alcohol layer. This is the DNA, and it will appear as a slimy, white mucus.

❹ If you like, you may collect the DNA with a wire hook or medicine dropper at the ethanol/filtrate interface. It's safe to touch, so go ahead and explore!

Interpreting Your Observations

What do you think is the purpose of each step in the extraction and precipitation of the DNA? The DNA here isn't pure; what other types of molecules might be present?

Facilitator's Guide
Fruitful DNA Extraction

Materials

for the whole group

▲ 70% or higher percentage ethanol, chilled overnight in a freezer

▲ light-colored detergent, such as dishwashing liquid

▲ balance

for each small group

▲ 1 500-mL or larger beaker, or 250-mL or larger flask

▲ 2 200-mL or larger graduated beakers

▲ 1 100-mL graduated cylinder

▲ 1 100-mL beaker

▲ a kiwi fruit

▲ knife and fork for cutting and mashing

▲ thermometer

▲ funnel

▲ basket-style paper coffee filter to fit in the funnel

▲ ice

▲ cold water

▲ hot tap water (60°C)

▲ 2 3-qt saucepans for water baths

▲ coffee stirrers

▲ 10 mL detergent

▲ 50 mL chilled ethanol

▲ 2 g table salt

▲ waxed paper or paper plate

▲ 1 test tube for each group member

▲ test tube rack or similar device

▲ 1 medicine dropper

▲ hook made from thin wire (optional)

▲ hot plate (optional)

Management

▲ Amount of time for the activity: 45 minutes

▲ Preparation time: 30 minutes

▲ Group size: 1–5

Preparation and Setup

Activity Overview

Extract DNA from kiwi fruit using simple household chemicals.

Concepts

❭ DNA is the genetic material in organisms.

❭ The sequence of DNA subunits determines an organism's traits.

❭ We can extract DNA from tissue using a very simple procedure.

Preparation

❶ Obtain the materials. Nearly pure ethanol (99–100%) works best. Less-pure ethanol can be purchased at some grocery stores, but be aware that it contains acetone as a denaturant and is extremely toxic. If neither of these forms of ethanol is unavailable, Bacardi 151 Rum (75.5% ethanol) works well as a substitute. If you choose to use this as your source of ethanol, be sure to conceal its identity.

❷ Chill the ethanol or ethanol substitute overnight in a freezer.

Questions for Getting Started

❭ Have you heard of DNA before? What does DNA do in living organisms?

❭ Do you look like your parents or siblings? Why do you think that this is so?

TIPS!

● The activity can be streamlined by preparing the extraction solution and hot and cold water baths ahead of time.

● The activity can be completed over a 2-day period. When most of the liquid has been filtered, the filtrate can be covered and stored in the refrigerator for use the next day. Or the entire filtration procedure may be conducted in a refrigerator overnight.

After the Exploration

Expected Results

A slimy white material will precipitate at the interface of the ethanol and filtrate layers. This material consists of clumped-together DNA strands and some protein.

What's Going On?

The procedure used in this activity has the same essential elements as more advanced laboratory DNA extraction procedures: mechanical and thermal disruption of cells, liberation of the DNA, and precipitation of the DNA.

In this procedure, the kiwi cell walls are broken down by the mechanical mashing and then the heating, and the detergent dissolves the lipids in the cell membranes and nuclear envelope (just like the detergent dissolves grease on your dishes). No longer confined inside nuclear membranes, the DNA—highly soluble in water because the phosphate group of each nucleotide carries a negative charge—goes into solution. However, the positively charged sodium ions from the salt in the extraction solution are attracted to the negatively charged phosphate groups on the DNA backbone, effectively neutralizing the DNA's electric charge. This neutralization allows the DNA molecules to aggregate with one another. When the ethanol is added, the DNA clumps together and precipitates at the water/ethanol interface because the DNA is not soluble in ethanol.

Each glob of material in the precipitate will contain millions of DNA strands clumped together, along with some of the protein that is normally associated with DNA. (Since the DNA was not highly purified, some protein precipitates out with the DNA.)

It is possible to analyze the extracted DNA in a research laboratory to provide good evidence that it really is DNA.

Each type of molecule, because of its unique structure, has a characteristic pattern of absorption of the electromagnetic spectrum. This pattern can be determined by an instrument called a spectrophotometer, which shines light of specific wavelengths through substances and records the degree of absorbance for each wavelength. DNA exhibits maximal absorbance at approximately 260 nm, while a typical protein shows peak absorbance at 280 nm. This difference can be used to distinguish the two types of molecules.

Kiwi fruit DNA extracted by the procedure outlined here was removed from solution, dissolved in a buffer, and subjected to spectrophotometric analysis in order to obtain a crude idea of its constituents and purity. The material showed an absorbance peak at 264 nm, indicating that it likely contains DNA with some contaminating protein.

Discussion Questions

❶ We can't isolate and touch most of the other molecules that make up living things as easily as we can the DNA from kiwi fruit cells. Why do you think this is so?

❷ Have you heard of the Human Genome Project? What is it and why is it important?

❸ Some people are concerned that we may be able to manipulate the DNA of people and that it will change them into something that they are not. Can you give some examples of the types of human genes that might be changed? Do you think that scientists should proceed with this type of research? Why or why not?

Going Further: Ideas for Inquiry

❭ Try to extract DNA from other fruits or vegetables using this procedure.

❭ Research and try other types of DNA extraction procedures. Compare the yield of another procedure with the yield from the one described here.

❭ Calculate how many times to the moon and back a human's DNA would reach if it was removed from each cell and each strand laid end-to-end. Here is the information you need: Each cell nucleus in a human holds about 2 meters of DNA and a typical adult human is composed of 60 trillion cells. The distance from the earth to the moon is 380,000 kilometers.

The Basics and Beyond

Background

Deoxyribonucleic acid (DNA) is the genetic material present in all organisms, from bacteria to humans. A single subunit of DNA is called a nucleotide and consists of a nitrogen-containing base, a sugar, and a phosphate group. Hundreds of thousands of nucleotides are hooked together to form a chain, and two chains are paired together and twisted into a double helix to form the finished DNA molecule (see Figure 1). In organisms with nucleated cells such as humans, DNA is coupled with protein in structures called chromosomes that are contained within a membrane-bound nucleus inside a cell.

Very pure DNA can be easily extracted from cells in a research laboratory, and somewhat less-pure DNA can be extracted with some simple techniques easily performed at home or in the classroom.

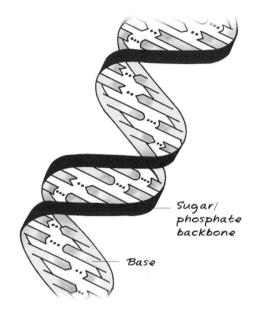

Figure 1: DNA double helix

Tidbits

❯ There are about 3×10^9 nucleotide base pairs in the human genome (the complete set of genes in one cell). If you took all of the DNA from a single human cell and laid the strands end to end, it would be about 2 meters long!

❯ All of that DNA is folded and packed into the nucleus of a human cell. The diameter of the nucleus is about 0.005 mm or $\frac{1}{500}$ the width of a dime.

❯ There are 6 billion bits of information coded by DNA in each of our nucleated cells (a bit is a measure of information). Each human cell contains twenty-one times the information that is found in the *Encyclopædia Britannica,* which is thought to have about 280 million letters.

Acknowledgment

Thanks to Dr. Robert Swezey of SRI International, Menlo Park, CA, for determining the absorption spectra of our DNA extracts.

Explorer's Guide

What You Can't See *Can* Hurt You

Experiment with an unseen form of energy that affects your body

We're surrounded by all kinds of invisible things on our bodies and in our environment. Most are harmless, but a few could injure us if given the opportunity. Find out about one of them and how you can protect yourself from its harmful effects.

Things You Will Need

▲ string of special beads
▲ 1 container with special beads

▲ access to materials you can use for experimenting with the beads
▲ paper for recording observations

To Do and Notice

This activity works best with a facilitator.

Observing

❶ Begin this exploration in a room lit only with artificial lighting. Observe the string of beads. Write a description of the beads including their color. Are they all the same?

❷ Take your string of beads outside. Observe the beads under the new conditions. Are there any changes? What are they?

❸ Go back indoors. Continue to observe the beads over the next few minutes. Are there any changes?

❹ Form a hypothesis about what's causing the changes in the beads. Share your ideas and discuss them with others.

Experimenting

❶ Figure out ways to test your hypothesis. Use any of the materials provided. If you cover the bead-filled container with plastic wrap, you can experiment with sunscreen. Record descriptions of your tests and all of the observations you make during your testing.

❷ If your experiments fail to support your hypothesis, form another and test it.

Interpreting Your Observations

What did you learn from your experiments? What factor causes the beads to change color? If you can't name this factor, how would you describe it? What sorts of factors might be difficult to test?

Facilitator's Guide
What You Can't See *Can* Hurt You

Materials

for the whole group

▲ UV-sensitive beads (1 string of about 6 beads for each explorer)

▲ materials to use for experimenting with the beads (see Preparation)

▲ material on which to string beads (e.g., pipe cleaners, yarn, string)

▲ paper or foam cups or black plastic film cans

▲ glue

▲ clear plastic wrap

for each small group

▲ string of UV-sensitive beads

▲ 1 paper or foam cup or film can filled with UV-sensitive beads

▲ access to materials for experimenting

▲ paper for recording observations

Management

▲ Amount of time for the activity: 40–50 minutes

▲ Preparation time: 30 minutes

▲ Group size: 1–4

| Preparation and Setup

Activity Overview

Experiment with UV-sensitive beads to determine what factor causes them to turn from pale to brightly colored.

Concepts

❯ The sun emits a range of electromagnetic radiation, some of which is visible and some of which is invisible.

❯ The characteristics of radiation depend on its wavelength.

❯ Ultraviolet light, which has a shorter wavelength than visible light, can cause sunburn and contribute to skin cancer.

❯ The skin can be shielded from the negative effects of ultraviolet light.

Preparation

❶ Obtain the UV-sensitive beads. A package of about 240 beads can be purchased inexpensively from Educational Innovations, Inc. (151 River Road, Cos Cob, CT 06807; phone toll free 1-888-912-7474)

❷ String the beads into an appropriate number of strands.

❸ Make bead-filled testing cups: Cut off the tops of the cups or film cans until they are about 1.5 cm tall from the base. Glue one layer of beads onto the bottom of each cup or can. Cover the beads with plastic wrap to create a surface on which sunscreen can be spread.

> ### Tips!
> ● Encourage the explorers to come up with as many possibilities as they can, then discuss which are testable and why. Encourage them to do the experiments if possible.
>
> ● Determining that sunlight causes the change in the beads is different from determining that an invisible component of sunlight, namely UV radiation, is what produces the change. Unless some investigators already know about UV radiation, the facilitator may have to provide this information. If you have access to a black light or other source of UV light, you can use it to show that UV light causes a color change in the beads whereas regular indoor lighting does not.

❹ Obtain materials for experimenting with the beads. You should have a variety of translucent and transparent materials, some which must absorb UV light, such as coated sunglasses, UV filters for camera lenses, and sunscreens. You may want to choose sunglasses or lens filters that have labels explicitly stating their UV-shielding properties. Materials without UV-shielding properties that you may want to provide include plastic transparencies, uncoated sunglasses, and regular glass. Also have on hand materials that could be used for testing non-UV effects (e.g., hot and cold water to test temperature effects or a fan to test the effect of the wind).

❺ Make sure the room in which the activity is carried out is not open to sunlight or bright outdoor light. Draw the blinds or cover the windows if necessary.

Questions for Getting Started

❯ What causes sunburn? What happens to your skin when you get sunburned?

❯ What do radio waves, microwaves, and X rays have in common?

After the Exploration

Expected Results

The beads will turn from white or pale pastel to bright colors when exposed to sunlight, and the bright colors will fade when the beads are taken out of the light. Artificial indoor light will not cause any change in the beads.

After experimenting with the various materials, investigators should be able to determine that some component of sunlight causes the beads to change color. Materials that allow some light to pass through them, such as some sunglasses and sunscreens, are as effective as opaque objects in preventing sunlight from causing colors to change.

What's Going On?

Ultraviolet rays from the sun (or a black-light fixture) interact with a UV-sensitive pigment in the beads to turn them bright colors. The energy in the ultraviolet light is absorbed by the pigment molecules in the beads. This elevates electrons in the pigment to a higher energy level, changing certain properties of the pigment, including its color. When the beads are shielded from ultraviolet light, the electrons gradually return to their normal energy levels and the beads change back to their pale colors.

Sunscreens and the coatings on some sunglasses are effective barriers to UV radiation because they contain molecules that absorb, and thus intercept, UV radiation. Materials such as regular glass and clear plastic allow the longer wavelengths of UV radiation to pass through.

Like the beads, unprotected skin cells absorb UV radiation, and the energy excites electrons in the molecules of the cells. But unlike the beads, unprotected skin cells are damaged after a certain amount of UV exposure. The reddish color that signals sunburn in light-skinned people is an indicator of cell damage. Darker-skinned people do not sunburn as easily because their skin is protected by a natural sunscreen. Dark skin contains a large amount of the pigment melanin, which absorbs UV radiation and thus protects skin cells from its damaging effects. (Nevertheless, darkly pigmented skin can be damaged by frequent or lengthy exposure to sunlight, especially where UV radiation is more intense, such as near the equator and at high elevation.)

UV radiation is absorbed by the DNA in the nuclei of unprotected skin cells. The resulting excitement of electrons in the DNA can damage it; if this damage is not repaired by the cell, it can lead to skin cancer.

Discussion Questions

❶ What do you do to protect your skin from UV radiation?

❷ Does being in or near the water or on snow affect the rate at which we suntan or sunburn? Why do you think this is so?

❸ The ozone layer of the atmosphere absorbs much of the ultraviolet radiation from the sun. How might the thinning of the ozone layer affect living organisms on earth? Have you heard of any effects already being observed?

Going Further: Ideas for Inquiry

❯ Use the beads to test sunscreens with different SPF values. Under sunscreens with widely different strengths (e.g., SPF 5 vs. SPF 30), the beads should show noticeable differences in color intensity.

❯ Use the beads to test the UV-shielding abilities of car windows. In general, windshields, which are specially treated, are good UV barriers, but side windows are not.

❯ Compare the reaction of the beads on a sunny day and a cloudy day. If there's a difference, what do you think accounts for it?

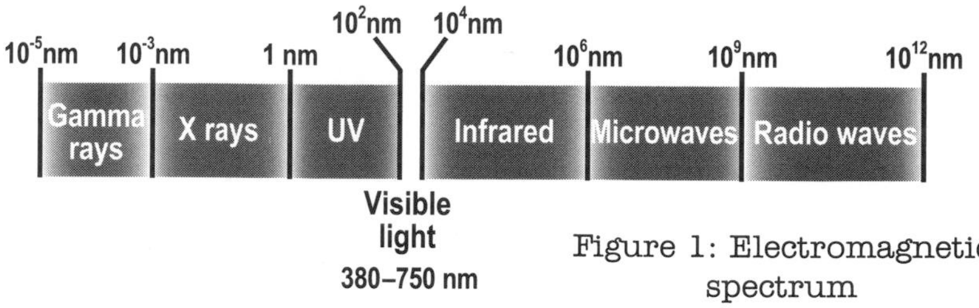

Figure 1: Electromagnetic spectrum

The Basics and Beyond

Background

Radiation from the sun affects humans in many ways. It warms the earth, affects our daily rhythms and moods, and sunburns light-colored skin (and even darkly pigmented skin with enough exposure). Each of these effects is actually the result of a different form of solar radiation with a particular range of wavelengths.

Visible light, which has wavelengths between 380 and 750 nanometers (nm), makes up only a small portion of the range of solar radiation (see Figure 1). Visible light is what affects our daily rhythms and moods. Solar radiation with a wavelength longer than that of visible light includes infrared light, microwaves, and radio waves. Infrared light is what warms the earth. At the opposite end of the spectrum are forms of short-wavelength, high-energy radiation such as X rays, gamma rays, and ultraviolet (UV) radiation. Ultraviolet radiation is what causes sunburn; it can also damage the DNA in skin cells, which can lead to skin cancer.

We cannot detect UV radiation with our eyes, but the plastic beads used in this activity respond quickly to UV exposure and can therefore be used to investigate ways of blocking UV radiation.

Tidbits

❯ Two forms of ultraviolet radiation reach the earth, UV-A (320–400 nm) and UV-B (290–320 nm). Ten to one hundred times more UV-A than UV-B reaches the earth.

❯ UV-A causes tanning, but also causes premature aging of the skin and is linked to skin cancer. UV-B is also linked to skin cancer because it is easily absorbed by DNA.

❯ The front of the eye absorbs more than 99% of the ultraviolet radiation it encounters. Repeated exposure over a long period of time can lead to cataracts and other eye disorders.

❯ Exposure to ultraviolet radiation allows the skin to synthesize vitamin D. However, in developed countries, most people meet their needs for vitamin D through their diets and don't need UV exposure.

❯ People who have the genetic disorder xeroderma pigmentosa must avoid all exposure to the sun. They lack the enzymes that repair certain types of DNA damage caused by exposure to the sun and therefore are very prone to skin cancer.

Explorer's Guide

The Domino Effect

Use dominoes to model a nerve cell's transmission of a signal

Your nervous system does its job by transmitting information through the long bodies of individual nerve cells as electrical impulses. Falling dominoes can simulate how a nerve cell is triggered and how it sends its impulse from one end of the cell to the other.

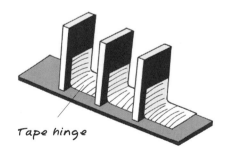

Figure 1A: Setup of dominoes with tape hinges

Figure 1B: Final setup of dominoes

Things You Will Need

▲ ruler, 30 cm or longer
▲ 8 standard dominoes
▲ masking tape
▲ scissors
▲ paper for recording observations

To Do and Notice

Constructing the Model

❶ Measure the length of one of your dominoes. Record the length.

❷ Cut 8 pieces of masking tape, each about the same length as a domino. (They don't need to be exact.)

❸ Place the first domino near the end of the ruler. Use a piece of masking tape to make a hinge connecting the back of the domino to the ruler. Figure 1A shows what tape hinges should look like.

❹ Place the second domino on the ruler about three-quarters of a domino's length from the first domino.

❺ Connect the second domino to the ruler with a tape hinge like you did in step 3.

❻ Attach the remaining 6 dominoes in the same way.

❼ Cut 8 more strips of masking tape, each about the length of a domino.

❽ Use these pieces of tape to reinforce the hinges. Wrap each piece of tape around the ruler and the base of the tape hinge. The hinges shown in Figure 1B are reinforced in this way.

Exploring with the Model

❶ Place the ruler flat on your desk, and make sure all the dominoes are upright. If necessary, turn the ruler so that the faces of the dominoes are facing you.

❷ Flick the first domino with your finger to make it fall. Watch and record what happens.

❸ Repeat step 2. What do you have to do before you can flick the dominoes again?

❹ Make the dominoes fall several more times and closely observe their reaction each time. Do they all fall at the same speed? Can you make them fall in the reverse direction? Record your observations.

❺ Reset the dominoes so that they are upright. Barely touch the first domino with your finger. Record what happens. Do this again several times, using slowly increasing amounts of force on the first domino. Record your observations.

❻ Remove one domino from the middle of the ruler. Reset the dominoes so that they are on end. Flick the first domino. What happens?

Interpreting Observations

Compare the response of the dominoes when the first one in the line is just barely touched to when you used significant force to flick it. Can you think of a way this models our ability to perceive different stimuli (touch, smell, dim light, etc.)? Hint: Is there a minimum strength of stimulus we need to feel a feather touching our arm? When the dominoes all fall, do they reset themselves? What must happen for them to be in the starting position again? Hypothesize how this might represent something comparable to the way our nervous system functions. When a domino is removed from the center of the line, what happens when you do the exploration? Can you think of any disease or disorder that this might model?

Facilitator's Guide

The Domino Effect

Materials

for each individual or pair

▲ ruler, 30 cm or longer

▲ 8 dominoes (standard, wooden)

▲ masking tape

▲ scissors

▲ paper for recording observations

Management

▲ Amount of time for the activity: 30–40 minutes

▲ Preparation time: 10 minutes to set out materials

▲ Group size: 1–2

Preparation and Setup

Activity Overview

Construct a simple device that models several important aspects of the way a nerve impulse is propagated from dendrite to axon.

Concepts

❯ Nerve cells are called neurons.

❯ Neurons require a stimulus of a minimum strength to fire.

❯ The nerve impulse is propagated along the length of the nerve cell.

❯ After a neuron has fired, there is a refractory period during which it cannot fire.

❯ Neurons use energy to reset their resting state so that they can fire again.

Preparation

None, except for obtaining materials.

Questions for Getting Started

❯ Has your doctor ever checked your reflexes by tapping your knee with a hammer? What happens? What do you think is wrong if your knee doesn't jerk?

❯ What is your spinal cord and what does it do?

TIP!

● If time is short, you can prepare the models ahead of time, or you can construct a single, larger model on a meterstick and use it for a demonstration of nerve impulse propagation.

After the Exploration

Expected Results

When the first domino is toppled, it begins a chain reaction in which each subsequent domino is toppled until there are no more dominoes to topple. This chain reaction has certain properties that can be related to the propagation of an impulse along the membrane of a neuron: The first domino must be pushed a certain distance before it will fall; the pulse of falling dominoes moves at a constant speed without losing energy as it travels; the pulse travels in one direction only; dominoes fall in an all-or-nothing fashion; energy must be used to reset the dominoes between each trial.

What's Going On?

Each property of the model noted above is analogous to an important aspect of neuron function:

❯ The first domino will not fall until it is pushed beyond a critical angle; in a similar way, a nerve impulse will not be triggered until the nerve is excited beyond its firing threshold. The threshold phenomenon can be seen in the operation of our sensory nerves: we cannot hear very faint sounds, for example, because the stimulus is not strong enough to excite the auditory nerve.

❯ Once the pulse of falling dominoes begins to propagate, it moves at a constant speed independent of the size of the starting push; analogously, the speed of the propagation of a nerve impulse is independent of the size of the triggering signal.

❯ The domino pulse does not lose energy as it propagates because the potential energy of each standing domino is released as kinetic energy when the domino falls; similarly, nerve impulses do not lose energy as they propagate.

❯ The domino pulse travels in only one direction; likewise, nerve impulses can travel only in the dendrite-to-axon direction.

❯ The dominoes cannot fall again until they are reset, which requires an input of human energy. In the same way, the nerve cell uses energy to redistribute ions and re-establish the resting state after a nerve impulse has propagated down the axon, and the nerve cannot fire again until this ▶ occurs.

The removal of a domino from the ruler models the effects of the disease multiple sclerosis. Just as the pulse of tumbling dominoes stops when it reaches the gap in the center of the ruler, a nerve impulse stops when it reaches a portion of a neuron damaged by multiple sclerosis.

The axons of neurons in the peripheral nervous system (sensory and motor neurons) are coated with a material called myelin. Myelin acts as an insulator similar to the nonconductive coatings of electrical wires. The insulation provided by myelin greatly increases the rate of conduction of nerve impulses. Unmyelinated nerves conduct impulses at about 1 mile per hour (0.5 m/s), but myelinated nerves transmit impulses at about 200 miles per hour (120 m/s).

In multiple sclerosis, the myelin sheaths are broken down, creating gaps in the myelin similar to holes in the insulation surrounding an electrical wire. These gaps interrupt the propagation of nerve impulses.

The removal of a domino also mimics the effects of a severe nerve or spinal cord injury. A nerve impulse cannot propagate past the site of the injury, just as the pulse of falling dominoes is stopped by the missing domino.

Discussion Questions

❶ Why do you think nerve impulses travel in only one direction?

❷ Do we feel everything that touches us? What are some things that might touch us that we don't feel? How would you explain this observation using the model?

❸ Sometimes people become paralyzed due to injuries from serious automobile or motorcycle accidents. What do you think causes the paralysis? Can you use the domino model to explain the reason for the paralysis?

Going Further: Ideas for Inquiry

❯ Find out how nerve impulses are transmitted between individual neurons, across the gap called the synapse. Explain how the dominoes can model this process as well.

❯ There are sounds you can't hear because they aren't strong enough to trigger the neurons in your inner ear. In the same way, there are tastes you can't taste, aromas you can't smell, and touches you can't feel. How strong does a stimulus have to be to trigger the neurons that allow you to experience touch, sight, sound, taste, and smell? Design some experiments to test the threshold level of the stimuli for one or more of your senses.

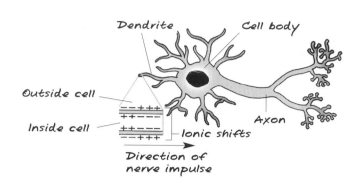

Figure 2: Changes in ions across a nerve cell membrane

The Basics and Beyond

Background

Nerve cells, or neurons, make up the information highways of the body. The job of most individual neurons is to pick up signals from neighboring neurons and transmit them to another neuron or to a target cell.

A neuron has three major regions: branched projections called dendrites; a central portion, the cell body, which contains the cell nucleus; and a single long projection called the axon (see Figure 2).

In a neuron at rest, the concentration of negative ions inside the neuron is greater than the concentration outside, creating a difference in charge across the neuron's plasma membrane. This difference in charge is called the membrane potential.

A sufficiently strong stimulus to the dendrite of a neuron initiates a nerve impulse. The impulse begins as an exchange of ions across a localized area of the plasma membrane, which reverses the polarity of the membrane potential there. This change is an all-or-nothing response and does not vary in intensity. This reversal of polarity causes the same change in the neighboring area of the membrane, which causes a reversal of polarity further along, and so on. In this way, the impulse propagates along the length of the neuron as a cascade of ionic exchanges. It does not lose energy as it travels because it is continually regenerated at each new site along the membrane. The impulse travels to the neuron's axon, which passes the signal on to another neuron or to a target cell by releasing chemicals called neurotransmitters.

Tidbit

❯ Axons can be very long—up to a meter in the case of a neuron that reaches from the big toe to the base of the spinal cord.

Explorer's Guide

You've Got Your Nerve!

Ordinary beans can model the ions in nerve cells

Do you remember the last time you touched a hot stove? You pulled your hand away immediately because it hurt! The heat caused nerve cells in your fingertip to fire: "gates" in the nerve cells opened, ions flowed through the gates, and the movement of ions began an electrical impulse that ultimately caused you to move your hand. Find out how your nerve cells make these important electrical impulses.

Things You Will Need

▲ 1 large bag of beans containing a small bag of beans

▲ paper for recording data

To Do and Notice

This activity works best with a facilitator.

❶ Notice the distribution of the beans in your plastic bags. How are the two bags different?

The beans inside the small, inner bag represent the ions inside a nerve cell. The beans in the large bag represent the ions outside of the cell. Each type of bean represents a certain kind of ion with a certain charge, as shown in Table 1. The way the beans are now represents a neuron at rest.

Table 1

Bean	Ion Represented	Charge
Lima	Large anions (A^-)	−2
Black	Sodium (Na^+)	+1
Red	Potassium (K^+)	+1
Pinto	Chloride (Cl^-)	−1

❷ You will be calculating the total charge inside and outside your "neuron" three times: as it is now, after moving some beans around, and again after moving other beans. To make this process easier, you can create a data table ahead of time. Read through the steps below to get an idea of what rows and columns to include in your table. You will want to have spaces in your table for recording the number of each kind of "ion" and for the total charge of this ion.

❸ Count and record the number of "large anions" (lima beans) inside the "neuron." Multiply this number by the charge of each large anion (−2) to find the total charge of the large anions inside the neuron. Record the total charge.

❹ Repeat step 3 for each of the three other types of "ions" inside the "neuron."

❺ Find and record the sum of the charges inside the neuron by adding up the positive and negative charges represented by the four kinds of ions.

❻ Count and record the number and total charge of each kind of ion outside the neuron.

❼ Find and record the sum of the charges outside the neuron by adding up the positive and negative charges represented by the four kinds of ions.

❽ Find the difference between the charge inside the neuron and the charge outside the neuron. This difference is the neuron's resting membrane potential. Record it in your data table. **Note:** The difference between the two charges is not their arithmetic sum! It is the distance between them. For example, if the charge inside the neuron is −6 and the charge outside is +7, the difference between them is 13, not 1.

❾ Determine if the resting membrane potential is positive or negative. The sign should be negative if the charge inside the cell is lower than the charge outside the cell; it should be positive if the charge inside the cell is greater than the charge outside the cell. Determine the sign and put it in front of the number you recorded for the resting membrane potential.

Now imagine that you touch a hot stove. A neuron in your finger starts a nerve impulse. This impulse travels to your spinal cord and back to your hand through several neurons.

In each neuron, the impulse travels as a moving change in the resting potential along the neuron's membrane. At each point along the membrane, a series of changes happens that you are about to model.

⑩ Move 15 sodium ions (black beans) from outside the neuron (large bag) to the inside of the neuron (small bag).

This movement represents what happens when sodium gates in the plasma membrane open and allow sodium ions to diffuse from the outside of the cell (the large bag) to the inside (the small bag). This movement causes a small part of the membrane to depolarize, a change in the membrane potential called the action potential.

⑪ Calculate the new membrane potential that results from this movement of sodium ions. Do this by repeating the process you followed in steps 3–9.

⑫ Move 15 potassium ions (red beans) from the inside of the cell to the outside.

This movement represents the next change that occurs in the cell membrane: the opening of the potassium gates and the closing of the sodium gates. As potassium ions diffuse out of the cell through their gates, the membrane potential changes once again. This process is called repolarization.

⑬ Calculate the membrane potential that exists after repolarization.

⑭ Finally, move 15 sodium ions (black beans) from the inside of the cell to the outside, and move 15 potassium ions (red beans) from the outside of the cell to the inside.

This final movement of ions puts all the ions (beans) back to where they were before the action potential occurred. The same process occurs in an actual neuron.

⑮ Seal the small bag, place it inside the large bag, and seal the large bag.

Analyzing Data and Drawing Conclusions

How does the membrane potential after depolarization compare to the membrane potential in the resting state? What happens to the membrane potential after repolarization? Is the distribution of ions after repolarization the same at it was in the initial resting state? If not, how is it different?

Facilitator's Guide

You've Got Your Nerve!

Materials

for the whole group

▲ large clear plastic zipper bags
▲ small clear plastic zipper bags
▲ black beans
▲ red beans
▲ pinto beans
▲ lima beans

for each pair or small group

▲ 1 bean-bag model, consisting of a small bag of beans within a large bag of beans (see Preparation)
▲ paper for recording data

Management

▲ Amount of time for the activity: 20–30 minutes
▲ Preparation time: 1 hour to set up the beans in the bags (first time only)
▲ Group size: 1–3+

TIPS!

● Complete "The Domino Effect" on page 75 before doing this activity.

● This activity can be simplified by using one type of bean to represent all the negative ions and another type to represent all the positive ions.

Preparation and Setup

Activity Overview

Using beans to represent the different ions that exist inside and outside a neuron, model the ionic shifts that occur across the cell membrane in the rapid change from resting potential to action potential and back again.

Concepts

❯ The inside of a neuron has a different distribution of ions than the fluid outside the cell, giving the cell a resting membrane potential.

❯ Rapid movement of certain ions across a neuron's plasma membrane depolarizes the membrane potential, creating an action potential.

❯ Sequential depolarization of the membrane along a neuron is what makes up a nerve impulse.

Preparation

❶ Obtain the materials. Each model requires 33 black beans (representing sodium), 31 red beans (potassium), 26 pinto beans (chloride), and 20 lima beans (large anions).

❷ Make the small bags of beans for the models: In each small zipper plastic bag, place the following set of beans:

3 black beans	30 red beans
2 pinto beans	20 lima beans

❸ Make the large bags of beans for the models: In each large zipper plastic bag, place the following set of beans:

30 black beans	1 red bean	24 pinto beans

❹ Seal each small plastic bag, and place it inside a large plastic bag along with its beans. Seal the large plastic bag.

Questions for Getting Started

❯ Why does electricity flow from one electrode of a battery to the other?

❯ What types of ions are inside a cell? Outside a cell?

After the Exploration

Expected Results

The table below summarizes what explorers should observe about the bean bag model during each of the three states:

Table 2

	Ion	Resting State Number of Ions	Resting State Total Charge	Depolarization Number of Ions	Depolarization Total Charge	Repolarization Number of Ions	Repolarization Total Charge
INSIDE cell	A^-	20	−40	20	−40	20	−40
	Na^+	3	+3	18	+18	18	+18
	K^+	30	+30	30	+30	15	+15
	Cl^-	2	−2	2	−2	2	−2
sum of charges			−9		+6		−9
OUTSIDE cell	A^-	0	0	0	0	0	0
	Na^+	30	+30	15	+15	15	+15
	K^+	1	+1	1	+1	16	+16
	Cl^-	24	−24	24	−24	24	−24
sum of charges			+7		−8		+7
Membrane potential			−16		+14		−16

What's Going On?

The number of beans of each ion type is directly proportional to the actual concentration of the ion inside or outside a nerve cell. Each bean represents a 5 millimolar (mM) concentration. The actual concentrations of the ion types (in mM) on each side of a neuron's membrane during the resting state are shown in Table 3.

After the repolarization, the resting membrane potential has been restored, but the concentrations of sodium and potassium ions have been reversed. Before the neuron can fire again, the original ionic concentrations must be restored. In a real neuron, "pumps" in the plasma membrane use energy to restore their ions to their starting concentrations. Here, explorers move the beans to return to the starting point.

Discussion Questions

❶ What would happen if a stimulus were received by an area of a neuron before it had been reset to its resting membrane potential?

❷ Do you think that drug or alcohol use might influence the speed of a nerve impulse along a nerve? How about lack of sleep or aging?

Table 3

Ion	Inside the Cell (mM)	Outside the Cell (mM)
A^-	100	0
Na^+	15	150
K^+	150	5
Cl^-	10	120

(The large anion category, A^-, is a catch-all group representing many kinds of macromolecules, each typically having a great many negative charges. The negative 2 charge is a simple way to represent these molecules.)

Going Further: Ideas for Inquiry

❯ Design experiments to compare the speed of nerve impulses in reflexes with the speed of nerve impulses in nonreflex responses.

The Basics and Beyond

Background

Nerve cells, or neurons, transmit information in electrical signals called nerve impulses. A nerve impulse travels the length of a neuron, from a dendrite to the axon. The impulse moves along the neuron as a pulse of electrical potential, propagated by changes in the neuron's cell membrane. At each location on the cell membrane, the same process occurs as the nerve impulse arrives, triggers changes, and is passed along the membrane. This activity focuses on what occurs during these changes in the membrane.

The distribution of ions and charged molecules is different inside and outside a neuron. Inside there are many large molecules, such as proteins and DNA, with negative charges. And compared to the extracellular fluid, the interior of the cell contains a much lower concentration of sodium ions (Na^+) and a much higher concentration of potassium ions (K^+). As a result of these differences, the interior is more negatively charged than the exterior (see Figure 1), creating an electrical potential with a measurable voltage.

When a neuron is not transmitting a nerve impulse, it is at rest; the difference in electrical charge across its membrane is called the resting membrane potential, and is about −70 millivolts (mV).

When a nerve impulse is propagated across an area of a neuron's membrane, the resting membrane potential at that location is changed by a redistribution of ions in the cell. Specialized "gates" for sodium and potassium, embedded within the membrane, open and close in sequence, allowing these ions to move across the membrane. The resulting depolarization of the membrane potential is called an action potential. Depolarization in one location on the membrane triggers depolarization in the adjacent part of the membrane, carrying the nerve impulse along the neuron.

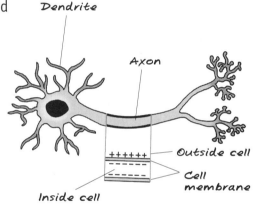

Figure 1: Diagram of neuron showing charges inside and outside the cell

Tidbits

❯ Each cell in an organism has a membrane potential, but only nerve cells and muscle cells use this potential to propagate electrical impulses.

❯ The average length of time that it takes a small area of a neuron's membrane to depolarize, repolarize, and use the sodium/potassium pump to return to the resting state is only 7 milliseconds (0.007 seconds).

Explorer's Guide

The Arctic in a Cup

Find out which materials are best at keeping you warm

You have to bundle up to go outside comfortably on a cold winter day, yet many animals live outside without the advantage of blankets and sweaters. Test the insulating abilities of several different materials, and learn more about how humans, and other warm-blooded animals, stay warm.

Things You Will Need

- ▲ 2 large foam cups
- ▲ 2 small paper cups
- ▲ 2 thermometers
- ▲ 2 thermometer holders
- ▲ tape
- ▲ water and ice
- ▲ insulating materials
- ▲ a clock
- ▲ paper towels
- ▲ paper for recording data

To Do and Notice

❶ Make two ice baths in the foam cups by filling them half-full with crushed ice and adding water until the cups are about two-thirds full. Add a thermometer to each and let the ice bath sit for at least 5 minutes to allow the temperature to stabilize. Check the temperature every 2 minutes.

❷ While the temperature of the ice baths is stabilizing, set up your first experiment: Choose two insulating materials. Based on your prior experience with these materials, predict which will insulate better and why. Then fill each paper cup with one of the insulating materials. Place a cardboard thermometer holder on top of each filled paper cup. Tape the holders securely to the cups.

❸ Get a sheet of paper to record the data from this investigation. After the temperature of the ice baths hasn't changed in two successive checks, record the temperature of the baths.

❹ Remove the thermometers from the ice baths and allow the thermometers to return to room temperature.

❺ Place each thermometer into one of the cups from step 2 by pushing it through the hole in the cardboard holder. The thermometer should fit very snugly in the hole. Position the thermometer so that the bulb (the bottom of the thermometer) is in the very center of the paper cup, as shown in Figure 1. If the thermometer is touching the bottom, your results may not be easy to interpret! Record the starting temperature inside each paper cup.

❻ Place each paper cup inside an ice bath. Record the time. Make sure that each cup is mostly submerged in its ice bath. You may need to hold the cup down in the ice bath if it floats.

❼ Let the paper cups sit in the ice baths for exactly 5 minutes. Then take the temperature inside each paper cup and record it. How did the temperature inside of each paper cup change? Which material was the better insulator?

❽ If there's time, repeat the experiment with two different insulating materials and record the results.

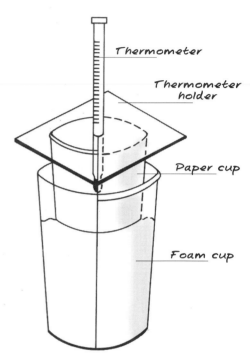

Figure 1: Setup of experimental apparatus

Analyzing Data and Drawing Conclusions

Which insulating material was the most effective? Use the data you recorded to explain your choice.

Displaying Data

Create a graph that shows the changes in temperature over time for all the materials.

Facilitator's Guide

The Arctic in a Cup

Materials

for the whole group

▲ a variety of insulating materials, such as lard (animal fat), dog fur, shredded paper, goose down, feathers, pieces of wool socks or blankets, Styrofoam™, packing material, pieces of neoprene

▲ crushed ice

▲ water

▲ clock with second hand

▲ thermometer to provide room temperature reading

▲ paper towels to mop up spills

for each pair

▲ 2 16-oz foam cups

▲ 2 6-oz paper cups

▲ 2 thermometers

▲ 2 cardboard thermometer holders

▲ tape

▲ ice, water, and insulating materials

▲ paper for data collection

Management

▲ Amount of time for the activity: 30–40 minutes

▲ Preparation time: 10 minutes to make the thermometer holders; 10 minutes to distribute materials. (You may want to have the participants make their own thermometer holders.)

▲ Group size: 2–4

Preparation and Setup

Activity Overview

Explore the effectiveness of a variety of insulating materials and determine which may work best in keeping the human body warm.

Concepts

❯ The body's core temperature cannot fall much below 36°C without serious consequences.

❯ A layer of fat under the skin helps to insulate the body against a colder outside environment.

❯ To supplement the fat layer, humans wear clothing that insulates by trapping air inside its fibers.

Preparation

❶ Obtain the necessary materials. One 3-lb can of lard will be enough for a group of 32. Dog fur can be obtained from a local dog groomer. Neoprene scraps can be obtained from many shops that sell or rent scuba diving equipment.

❷ Make thermometer holders: Cut a piece of cardboard to fit over the top of a paper cup. (Note that the cardboard doesn't have to be cut in a circle; a square slightly bigger than the opening of the cup works fine.) Poke a hole in the center of the cardboard so that a thermometer fits snugly through the hole. Make two of these per group—or have the participants make their own thermometer holders as part of the activity.

Questions for Getting Started

❯ What are some of the functions of fat in the human body?

❯ What are ways that you can dress to help keep you warm in cold weather?

> **TIP!**
> ● To provide a control in the experiment, several groups can run trials in which they don't put any insulating material inside one of the cups.

After the Exploration

Discussion Questions

❶ Is air a good insulator? Why or why not? How could you test your hypothesis using today's exploration as a model?

❷ Images of models today glorify the ultrathin, nearly skeletal look for women. What are some of the health problems that are associated with trying to achieve this unrealistic body form?

Going Further: Ideas for Inquiry

❯ Pursue your own inquiries about this subject. Here are questions you might want to consider: At what rate does the temperature decrease for different materials? What steps can be taken to make sure that the different properties of materials are being compared, rather than different amounts of materials?

❯ Test the efficiency of insulation materials when they are immersed in water. Use buckets for the ice baths (scale up water and ice as necessary) and use quart-size sealable plastic bags to hold the insulating materials and thermometers. Water pressure will compress the materials as long as a small hole is left at the top of the bag and the bag isn't submerged all the way.

The Basics and Beyond

Background

The human body can function properly only when its core temperature is within a relatively narrow range. When the environmental temperature is cold, body heat must be conserved and several mechanisms come into play. The blood vessels in the skin constrict, minimizing heat loss while maintaining blood flow to vital body organs in the core. The body's metabolic rate increases, which generates heat as a by-product. Skeletal muscles contract involuntarily in a shudderlike manner, generating a lot of heat. These responses are controlled through the autonomic nervous system by a kind of thermostat located in the hypothalamus of the brain, which attempts to keep body temperature between 36.1°C and 37.8°C (97°F and 100°F). If the body's heat-conserving and heat-generating mechanisms aren't sufficient, the temperature of the body's core falls and hypothermia results, which may lead to coma and death.

In most of the world's climates, conserving body heat by insulating the body against the colder outside environment is a survival issue, at least during the winter season. The body itself provides one important source of insulation: a layer of adipose tissue, made up mostly of fat cells, located beneath the dermis of the skin.

Unlike other mammals, humans don't have an additional insulating layer provided by fur; and unlike birds, we don't have a layer of feathers. Both fur and feathers insulate by trapping air, which has relatively low thermal conductivity and is therefore an excellent insulator.

However, humans do take advantage of the insulating qualities of air by dressing in layers of clothes that trap air, and by wearing clothing stuffed with feathers or made out of fur. We also wear clothing made of synthetic fibers that trap air. By wearing layers of insulating materials, humans are able to live in and explore environments that would otherwise be deadly.

Expected Results

The materials will vary in their ability to insulate the thermometer from the cold. Fat, the major insulator of the human body, does a relatively good job, but in this experiment the temperature in the center of the cup is likely to decrease less with materials such as wool, feathers, or fur than it does with fat.

What's Going On?

Heat is energy that moves from a hotter area to a cooler area. In this exploration, or any time two bodies are in contact, heat moves by a process of conduction. Conduction occurs when more-energetic molecules collide with their less-energetic neighbors and pass on some of their kinetic energy in the process.

In this case, the space inside the cup is the warmer area and the ice bath is the cooler area. The different insulating materials placed in the paper cup limit—to varying degrees—the conductance of heat from the center of the cup (where the thermometer is) to the ice water. The transfer of heat is indicated by a decrease in the temperature inside the paper cup. You can think of the spot where the thermometer is located as a model for the body's core and the ice bath as the surrounding environment. Although the insulating materials slow down the conductance of heat, they cannot stop it; so if a cup were left in the ice water bath for long enough, its interior temperature would eventually reach equilibrium with the ice water.

Tidbits

❭ The thermal conductivity of a material is a constant (k) determined experimentally by a standard set of conditions. It is expressed as a measure of heat transfer in units of joules (or kilocalories) per second per meter per degrees Celsius. The higher the k value, the better the conductor of heat a material is; the lower the number, the better the insulator. At the right are some examples.

❭ Body fat may not insulate as well as fur or feathers, but it does have the advantage of being incompressible. When fur or feathers are immersed underwater, such as by diving animals, the fur and feathers are compressed and lose the layer of air that they normally trap, thus losing most of their insulating ability. Diving mammals such as seals and sea lions usually have a thick layer of blubber (fat) for insulation.

❭ Wet suits that scuba divers use to protect themselves from cold water are like an extra layer of fat; wet suits are made of a material called neoprene, which is not very compressible. Additionally, the wet suit has small air pockets embedded in the material to provide effective insulation.

❭ Fetuses, newborns, and infant humans have a special kind of fatty tissue not present in adults called brown fat. Brown fat cells have a high concentration of mitochondria that metabolize the fat in such a manner that much more heat is produced than from regular fatty tissue. This may be one reason that newborns don't shiver when exposed to the cold.

❭ When people lose much of their body fat, as in the disorder anorexia nervosa, the body often responds by growing hair over areas not normally covered with hair. It is believed that this response is an attempt to reestablish insulation of the body.

Material	k(J/s·m·C°)
Styrofoam	0.01
Air	0.02
Down	0.03
Wool	0.04
Cork	0.04
Asbestos	0.16
Body Fat	0.20
Water	0.56
Ice	2.00
Steel	45.00
Silver	410.00

Thermal conductivity of representative materials, in order from best to worst insulator

Part 2
Your Observable Body

Explorer's Guide
Tunnel of Light

Light entering one eye can affect what you see with your other eye

Have you ever noticed how the pupils of a cat's eyes respond to light? In the dark, the pupils are big and round, but in bright sunlight they are only narrow slits. Your eyes respond in a similar way, and each eye affects the other! Explore how this automatic adjustment system works.

Caution:
Make sure the light isn't bright enough to hurt your eyes.

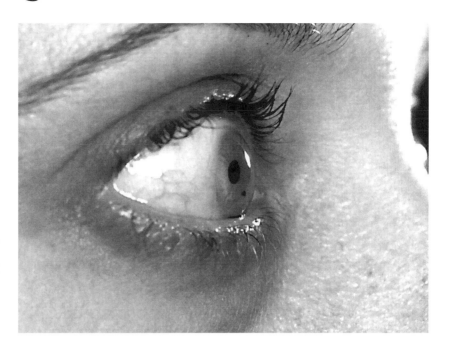

Things You Will Need

▲ a black plastic film can with a pinhole punched in its base

▲ access to a strong light source

To Do and Notice

❶ If your film can has a lid, remove it. Hold the film can up to your right eye with the open end resting on your eye socket. Remove glasses if applicable.

❷ Close your left eye. Look through the hole in the film can with your right eye. Look at a light. Pay attention to the hole. What do you see? Continue to focus on the hole and look at the light with your right eye for the next two steps.

❸ Open your left eye. Does anything you see with your right eye change?

❹ Now close your left eye. Are there any changes in what you see with your right eye?

❺ You may want to repeat this activity a few times, and then switch eyes.

Interpreting Your Observations

Does opening or closing the eye without the film can on it always cause a change in what the eye with the film can sees? What do your observations suggest about the relationship between your two eyes?

Facilitator's Guide

Tunnel of Light

Materials

for the whole group

- ▲ black plastic film cans
  (1 for each explorer)
- ▲ a push pin
- ▲ a strong light source
  (overhead room light or desk lamp)

for each individual

- ▲ a black film can with a pinhole
  in base
- ▲ access to a strong light source

Management

- ▲ Amount of time for the activity:
  10 minutes
- ▲ Preparation time: 10 minutes
- ▲ Group size: 1

Preparation and Setup

Activity Overview

Light entering one eye affects the size of the pupil in the other eye.

Concepts

❭ Light enters the interior of the eye through an opening called the pupil; the size of the pupil is controlled by the iris.

❭ When the eye is exposed to bright light, the iris immediately contracts, constricting the diameter of the pupil and lowering the amount of light entering the eye.

❭ Light entering only one eye can cause the iris of the other eye to contract, even if the other eye is not exposed to light.

Preparation

Use a push pin to poke a hole in the center of the bottom of each film can.

Questions for Getting Started

❭ Have you ever looked at a really bright light and had trouble seeing for a few seconds afterward? (Don't try this!) Why do you think this temporary blindness happens?

❭ What is a reflex? Can you control a reflex? Can you give some examples of reflexes?

TIPS!

● Film canisters are readily available from photographic stores. If you don't have any, however, it is possible to substitute squares of black construction paper with pinholes punched in them. The effect is less dramatic because stray light enters the eye from around the paper.

● To better see the reflex, it may help to darken the room except for the light source being used in the exploration.

After the Exploration

Expected Results

A circle of light is seen through the hole in the film can. When the left eye is opened, the circle appears to contract. When the left eye is closed again, the circle appears to enlarge. The response should be the same for either eye looking through the pinhole.

What's Going On?

The photopupillary reflex is causing the circle of light to change size. When the left eye opens, the sudden increase in light intensity entering this eye triggers the reflex, causing the pupils in both eyes to constrict. The circle grows smaller because the pupil in the right eye has become smaller. The circle grows again when the left eye is closed because the photopupillary reflex has dilated the right pupil.

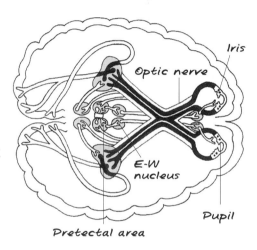

Figure 1: Pathway of the photopupillary reflex

The photopupillary reflex is controlled by a system of neurons separate from those responsible for the transmission and interpretation of visual images (see Figure 1). This system includes a few optic nerve fibers that carry information about light intensity from the right and left eyes to corresponding right and left pretectal areas of the midbrain. Nerves in just one pretectal area can transmit this information to the Edinger-Westphal (E-W) nuclei on both sides of the midbrain. Because both left and right E-W nuclei—the areas of the brain responsible for sending messages to the irises—are always activated, a light-intensity change in one eye will always affect both irises.

Discussion Questions

1 When someone has experienced a blow to the head, a doctor may shine a bright flashlight into one of the person's eyes to check for damage to the brain. Can you use your knowledge of the photopupillary reflex to explain how this test works?

2 The photopupillary reflex isn't sufficient to prevent damage to the retina if you look directly at the sun when it's at its brightest. Why do you think that this is so?

3 What other factors beside light can affect the size of your pupil?

Going Further: Ideas for Inquiry

❯ Modify this experiment to determine if the pupils dilate and constrict at exactly the same time, or if there's a lag period for reaction in the eye that is not exposed to the light.

The Basics and Beyond

Background

Light enters the eye through an opening called the pupil. The iris, a muscular ring that changes its diameter to control pupil size, ensures that light enters the eye at an optimum level. The midbrain, which receives information on the intensity of light entering the eyes, sends instructions to the irises to adjust their size accordingly. The resulting constriction and dilation of the pupil is called the photopupillary reflex. Like any reflex, this constriction is an automatic response that does not involve conscious thought.

Because the midbrain always sends its message to both irises, the photopupillary reflex occurs in both eyes—even if only one eye is suddenly exposed to bright light.

Tidbits

❯ There are about one million nerve fibers that make up each optic nerve. About 10% of these are involved in the control of pupil size, and in the eye and head movements needed to track moving objects.

❯ Receptor cells in the retina convert visual images to nerve impulses with the use of special light-sensitive chemicals. These chemicals are broken down when exposed to light, and don't function again until they are regenerated. When you look at a bright light, the chemicals are rapidly broken down and don't have a chance to regenerate, which explains why you may be temporarily blinded by bright light. Your vision is restored, however, if you close your eyes or go to a darker place and give the chemicals time to regenerate.

❯ During the Middle Ages, women enlarged their pupils by putting drops of a drug called belladonna (which means "beautiful woman" in Italian) into their eyes. The drug worked to dilate the pupils and make the eyes appear more luminous. The drug, used even in modern times, was finally banned by the FDA in the 1940s because it was so dangerous. It comes from the leaves and stems of the deadly nightshade plant, which contain atropine, an extremely poisonous alkaloid.

Explorer's Guide

Something in Your Eye

Illuminate the mysterious branching structure in your eye

In the back of your eye is a pattern that is as unique as your fingerprints. Like fingerprints, it can be used to establish your identity. Take an inside look and see the part of your eye that's uniquely you.

Things You Will Need

▲ penlight
▲ paper towel

▲ rubber band or tape

To Do and Notice

❶ Use two layers of paper towels to cover the end of the penlight. Secure the paper towels to the penlight with a rubber band or tape. The light coming from the penlight must be dimmed because you will be using it close to your eye.

❷ Hold the penlight below your line of vision, pointing upward at an angle toward the top of your eye. Make sure the paper-towel-covered end is about a centimeter from your lower eyelashes, as shown in Figure 1 on page 100. Turn on the light, but do not look directly into it. If the light hurts your eyes, use another layer of paper towel to decrease the intensity of the light, and test it to see if it is OK.

Before you complete the next steps, read and remember them, and then darken the room.

❸ If you wear glasses, remove them. Look across the room, and focus on a darkened wall. Hold the penlight as you did before, with the light source about one centimeter from your lower eyelashes. Turn on the light but, as before, don't look directly into it. Wiggle the light just a little bit.

❹ Keep focusing on the distant wall while the light is on. You are waiting for a "surprise" image to pop into your visual field. Sometimes it takes awhile to see this surprise. You may need to slowly adjust the distance of the light from your eye, change the angle of the penlight, or roll it slowly along your lower eyelashes. If at any time the light begins to hurt your eye, turn it off immediately.

Interpreting Your Observations

What did the image look like? What do you think it was?

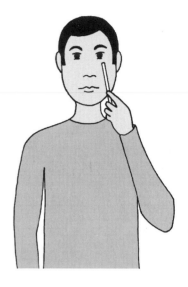

Figure 1: Positioning
of penlight

Facilitator's Guide

Something in Your Eye

Materials

for the whole group

▲ as many penlights as possible (up to 1 per explorer)

▲ supply of paper towels

▲ tape or supply of rubber bands

Management

▲ Amount of time for the activity: 15–20 minutes

▲ Preparation time: none

▲ Group size: 1 (with sharing of the modified penlights)

TIPS!

● Try this activity on yourself so that you may better assist explorers. Also enlist the help of those who can see the image. You may want to describe the branching pattern of the image without saying what causes it.

● Because of varying light intensity among penlights and varying opacity of paper towels, it's a good idea to test your penlights to find the optimum number of paper towel layers to use.

Preparation and Setup

Activity Overview

Use a penlight to view a mysterious branching image that's formed by the blood vessels serving the retina.

Concepts

❯ The retina is the layer of tissue at the back of the eyeball that contains light-sensing receptors.

❯ The blood supply to the retina lies in front of the retina, and consists of highly branching arteries, veins, and capillaries.

Preparation

None, except for obtaining materials.

Questions for Getting Started

❯ What part of the eye is responsible for converting images into nerve impulses that the brain can interpret?

❯ Are there blood vessels in your eye? How do you know?

After the Exploration

Expected Results

Explorers will see a network or branching pattern appear in their fields of vision. They will still be able to see other images through this image, which often appears slightly orange against a dark background.

What's Going On?

The branching pattern is formed by the blood vessels (arteries, veins, and capillaries) that serve the retina (see Figure 2). The light from the penlight enters the eye and passes through the layer of blood vessels before it hits the retina. Because the blood vessels absorb some of the light, they cast "shadows" on the retina. These shadows form the branching pattern.

Normally, we never see the retinal blood vessels or their shadows because they are always there and the brain ignores such unchanging images. But with the lights dimmed and a strong point source of light entering the eye, the shadows of the retinal blood vessels become visible.

Discussion Questions

❶ The lens and cornea of the eye do not have their own direct blood supply, but their cells do need oxygen. How do you suppose they obtain the necessary oxygen?

❷ Certain eye drops are supposed to "get the red out" of bloodshot eyes. What causes bloodshot eyes? How do you think the drops work?

Going Further: Ideas for Inquiry

❯ Explore other "invisible" things that float in front of your retina. On a clear day, stare at the blue sky, focus on it, and relax. After a few moments you should see something, or a collection of "somethings," in your field of vision. Find out what could be causing you to see these various shapes in your field of vision.

❯ Draw the pattern of your retinal blood vessels. Introduce family members and friends to this activity and ask them to draw the pattern of blood vessels that they see. Are they the same? Do people who are related show patterns more similar than unrelated people? Find out about using retinal scans for identification purposes.

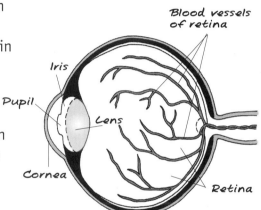

Figure 2: Cross section of human eye

The Basics and Beyond

Background

The retina is the layer of tissue at the back of the eye that contains light receptors called rods and cones. When light travels through the eye and hits the retina, the rods and cones convert the information contained in the light into neural impulses. The optic nerve carries these impulses to the brain for interpretation.

The cells of the retina need oxygen and nutrients delivered to them and waste products removed. This service is carried out by blood vessels that enter the eyeball along with the optic nerve. An artery known as the arteria centralis retinae branches into smaller vessels, forming a layer of capillaries in front of the retina. A network of veins is also part of this layer. These blood vessels are normally invisible, but under certain conditions the shadows they cast on the retina can be seen.

Tidbit

❯ Glaucoma is a disease of the eye in which pressure inside the eyeball builds up, squeezing the retinal blood vessels and reducing blood flow to the retinal cells. The reduced blood supply gradually causes the retinal cells to die, beginning at the periphery and moving in toward the center. Death of cells at the periphery of the retina results in tunnel vision, one of the classic symptoms of glaucoma.

References

Walker, Jearl. "Amateur Scientist." *Scientific American,* April 1982. (Features descriptions of strange things you can see in your own eyes.)

Explorer's Guide

A "Hole" New Experience

Even though it's inside your eye, you can figure out the size of your blind spot

Everyone has a hole in her or his vision called the blind spot. Without it we couldn't see at all! Explore this hole in your vision, and figure out just how big it is.

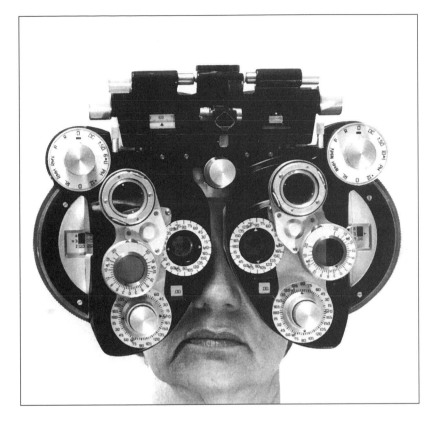

Things You Will Need

- ▲ 2 large sheets of paper
- ▲ tape
- ▲ bamboo skewer
- ▲ red sticky "dots" or red marker
- ▲ meterstick
- ▲ pencil
- ▲ paper for recording data

Caution:
The bamboo skewers have very sharp tips; be careful when you handle them.

To Do and Notice

You'll need a partner for this activity. Each of you will estimate the size of your blind spot using simple geometry.

You may want to create a data table before you begin the activity. In this table, your partner can record the measurements that will allow you to calculate the size of your blind spot. Read through the steps below to determine what rows and columns to use for your data table.

❶ With your partner, find a flat, blank space on a wall or cabinet. Tape a sheet of your paper to the wall so that the center is at eye height.

❷ Use a red marker or sticky dot to color the very tip of the bamboo skewer. The red part should be as thin as possible and no longer than half a centimeter.

❸ Choose who will be the volunteer and who will be the assistant. You will switch roles after the first volunteer completes three trials.

❹ At the volunteer's eye height, 15 to 20 cm to the left of the very center of the paper, make an X about 2.5 cm high.

❺ Volunteer: Stand up straight at arm's length from the paper. Place your hands flat against the paper, shoulder-height and shoulder-distance apart, with your fingers pointing up. Lock your elbows. Keep your face pointing straight ahead. Remember this placement of your head and shoulders. Maintain this position and try to keep your head as still as possible during this activity. You may now lower your arms to your side.

❻ Assistant: Notice the position of the volunteer's head and make sure it doesn't move. Ask the volunteer to close his or her eyes while you make a measurement. Being very careful of the volunteer's eye, use the meterstick to measure the distance in centimeters from the front of the volunteer's eye to the center of the paper. If the volunteer is wearing glasses, temporarily remove the glasses and measure the distance to his or her eye. Be sure that the meterstick is parallel to the ground. We will call this distance *D*. If the volunteer moves his or her head during the measurement, repeat step 5 and measure again. Record your measurement in the volunteer's data table.

Caution:
Be very careful of the volunteer's eye.

❼ Volunteer: Close your left eye and stare at the X on the paper with your right eye. Don't let your eye wander from the X and avoid moving your head. Keep your left eye shut until the end of this part of the activity.

❽ Assistant: Place the red tip of the skewer on the X. Move it slowly to the right in a straight line parallel to the floor. The volunteer must continue to stare at the X with his or her right eye.

❾ Volunteer: While focusing on the X with your right eye, tell the assistant exactly when you no longer see the red tip of the skewer (it will seem to magically disappear). Make sure you do not move your focus from the X!

❿ Assistant: Mark with a pencil the exact spot on the paper where the red tip left the volunteer's field of view.

⓫ Assistant: Continue to slowly move the tip of the skewer to the right.

⓬ Volunteer: Tell the assistant exactly when you see the red tip again. Assistant: Mark this spot on the paper.

You may have to repeat steps 7 through 12 to get it just right; that's fine, since your results should be as accurate as possible.

13 Measure the distance between the two marks on the paper in centimeters. We will call this distance *d*. Record this number in the volunteer's data table and erase the pencil marks.

14 Repeat steps 5–13 two more times with the same person as the volunteer. For each trial, record the measurements for *D* and *d*.

15 Switch roles. Using a new sheet of paper taped to the wall, do the activity three times and record the results for each trial in the new volunteer's data table.

Now you can calculate the size of your blind spot. Notice in Figure 1 that *D* and *d* form the altitude and base of an isosceles triangle. A similar triangle is formed inside your eye, with its base (*B*) being the diameter of your blind spot, and its altitude being about 2.5 cm. The bases and altitudes of these two triangles are proportional. Mathematically,

$$\frac{B}{2.5} = \frac{d}{D}$$

This equation can be expressed as a formula for finding the diameter of the blind spot:

$$B = \frac{2.5\,d}{D}$$

16 Use the formula above to calculate *B* for each trial for which you were the volunteer. Enter the values for *B* in your data table.

17 Now find the average value for *B* by adding up the values for the three trials and dividing by 3. The result is a good estimate of the size of your blind spot.

Analyzing Data and Drawing Conclusions

What is the size of your blind spot? How does it compare to the size of your retina as a whole? Why do you think your blind spot doesn't cause a "hole" in your field of vision?

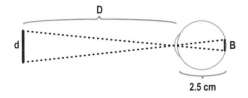

Figure 1: Top view of similar triangles

Facilitator's Guide

A "Hole" New Experience

Materials

for each pair

▲ 2 large sheets of butcher paper or other unlined paper (at least 65 cm wide)

▲ tape

▲ bamboo skewer

▲ red sticky "dots" or red marker

▲ meterstick

▲ pencil

▲ paper for recording data

Management

▲ Amount of time for the activity: 30–45 minutes

▲ Preparation time: none

▲ Group size: 2

Preparation and Setup

Activity Overview

Use perceptual skills and simple geometry to calculate the approximate size of the blind spots on retinas.

Concepts

❯ The optic nerve conveys information from the eye to the brain.

❯ At its point of attachment to the retina, the optic nerve creates a "blind spot" on the retina that cannot process the image that falls on it.

❯ Our brains "fill in" the image that falls on the blind spot based on the surrounding image.

Preparation

None, except for obtaining materials.

Questions for Getting Started

❯ What is the retina of the eye and what does it do?

❯ Trace the path of light as it enters your eye and hits the retina. What parts of the eye does the light pass through?

After the Exploration

Expected Results

The average size of the blind spot, or optic disk, is between 0.4 and 0.5 cm. Using the technique described in this exploration, it is possible to calculate this size quite accurately.

TIPS!

● It may help to demonstrate the activity with a volunteer.

● To get the most accurate measurement of the size of the blind spot in humans, collect all the calculated average sizes and use the median value among them to represent the large group's best estimate.

Some of the variation in the results may be due to error caused by incorrect head positioning. It is possible for a volunteer to hold his or her head so that the optic disk is measured across a point where the disk is not its widest (i.e., a chord above or below the diameter). Taking the average for three trials for each volunteer helps to minimize this kind of error.

What's Going On?

Objects viewed by the eye are projected as images on the retina. Because light from an object travels in straight lines and passes through the narrow opening of the pupil, the image on the retina is reversed in relation to what is being viewed. If we assume that the pupil and lens together behave like the pinhole in a pinhole camera, then the pupil is the common vertex of two similar triangles, the bases of which are the outside edges of the object being viewed and the width of the corresponding image projected on the retina.

The brain doesn't receive information about all of the image projected on the retina because the blind spot on the retina doesn't have photoreceptors. The brain "fills in" the missing part of the image by using information from the adjacent photoreceptors. In this activity, the volunteer perceives the paper that's taped to the wall but does not perceive the red mark on the skewer—which is consistent with the image on the photoreceptors near the optic disk.

The marks on the paper are an "image" of the blind spot. Each mark on the paper corresponds to an outside edge of the optic disk. Because of the principle of similar triangles, the distance between the two marks is proportional to the diameter of the disk. Knowing the base and altitude of the larger triangle and the altitude of the smaller triangle, the base of the smaller triangle—the diameter of the optic disk—can be calculated.

Discussion Questions

❶ Do you think that the blind spot on your retina ever contributes to clumsy behavior, such as bumping into something or dropping something thrown to you? Why or why not?

❷ Have you ever heard of a detached retina? What can cause it and what does it do to your vision?

Going Further: Ideas for Inquiry

❯ Perform the activity in the vertical (up-and-down) dimension by moving the skewer up from the X instead of to the right. Does the vertical diameter of the blind spot differ from its horizontal diameter?

❯ Conduct the activity on a larger scale by having the volunteer stand several meters away from a white wall while the assistant moves a small red object across the field of view.

The Basics and Beyond

Background

The back of the eye contains a light-sensitive tissue called the retina. Light that passes through the pupil forms an image on the retina and stimulates photoreceptors (light receptors) embedded there. Stimulated photoreceptors send nerve impulses to the optic nerve, which then conducts the information to the brain for interpretation.

The optic nerve is connected to the back of the eyeball, where it forms an area on the retina called the optic disk (see Figure 2). This is also the region that blood vessels enter and exit the eye. There are no photoreceptors in the optic disk; therefore, there's a "hole" in the image on the retina. Normally the missing information is picked up by the other eye. Even if we're looking at something with only one eye, however, we still don't perceive the hole. That's because the brain fills it in with information from the photoreceptors surrounding the optic disk.

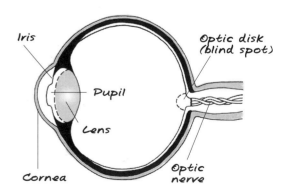

Figure 2: A side view of the human eye

Explorer's Guide

The Taste of Color

Should you trust your eyes or your sense of taste?

What color do you expect a juicy, sweet strawberry to be? Would you like to eat a blue banana? What do you think purple orange juice would taste like? Would green meat be safe to eat? Explore the connection between the color of food and your perception of its taste.

Things You Will Need

▲ paper plate
▲ fork or toothpick
▲ napkins
▲ access to 3 different flavors of gelatin
▲ glass of water
▲ paper for recording observations

To Do and Notice

This activity works best with a facilitator.

To keep this activity fun and suspenseful, don't discuss your results with anyone until you have recorded them! Each gelatin cube may or may not be the flavor that its color suggests. Don't let anyone else influence your "flavor vote."

You may want to prepare a table for your observations before you begin. Read through the steps below to determine the columns and rows your table should have.

❶ Obtain a cube of one of the three flavors of gelatin. Note whether it is A, B, or C. Observe the cube and record its color.

❷ Predict what the cube will taste like based on its color. Record your prediction.

❸ Taste the gelatin cube and determine its flavor. Record the flavor you perceive.

❹ Rinse your mouth with a little water and swallow before you taste the next sample.

❺ Repeat steps 1–4 for the two other flavors of gelatin.

❻ Find out the "true" flavor of each gelatin sample. Is each one the flavor you thought it was?

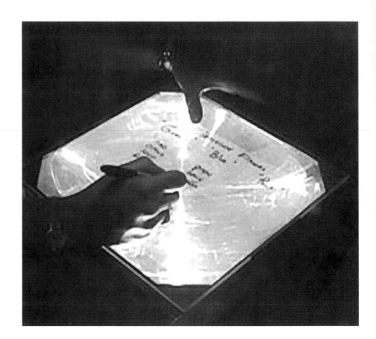

Interpreting Your Observations

What flavor did you expect each gelatin cube to be? Why did you anticipate that flavor? Did the flavor you tasted agree with your expectation, or did you taste a different flavor? Based on your observations, what can you conclude about the influence of our experiences on how we "taste" different foods?

Facilitator's Guide

The Taste of Color

Materials

for the whole group

▲ 3 flavors of gelatin dessert

▲ food coloring (at least 2 different colors)

▲ paper plates for serving

▲ plastic forks, toothpicks

▲ tongs, spoons, or forks for serving gelatin

▲ napkins

▲ drinking water

▲ glasses

for each individual

▲ paper plate

▲ fork or toothpick

▲ napkins

▲ access to 3 flavors of gelatin

▲ glass of water

▲ paper for recording observations

Management

▲ Amount of time for the activity: 30 minutes

▲ Preparation time: 30 minutes

▲ Group size: 1

Preparation and Setup

Activity Overview

Cubes of gelatin have been prepared so that their colors may not correspond to their flavors in the expected way. The flavors perceived when the gelatin's eaten illustrate how visual cues can influence sensory perception.

Concepts

❯ Because we learn to connect the taste of food to its color and appearance, certain visual cues create taste expectations.

❯ Expectations of taste, based on prior experience, can influence the perception of taste.

Preparation

❶ Obtain the gelatins and other materials. Regular gelatin with sugar works best; if you use sugar-free gelatin, the taste of the sweetener may be evident. Each 6-oz package of gelatin makes enough gelatin for a group of about fifty.

❷ Prepare the gelatins as directed on the packages. While still liquid, add food coloring to alter the color of two of the three flavors of gelatin (e.g., add red coloring to lemon gelatin). Label the three batches of gelatin A, B, and C, and record the (altered) color and flavor of each.

❸ When the gelatin is set, cut it into 2–3 cm cubes—at least one cube of each flavor per explorer. Transfer the cubes into labeled plastic containers for transport. Keep refrigerated until used.

❹ Set out the gelatin at three stations labeled A, B, and C.

Questions for Getting Started

❯ What is the flavor of a red soda? A brown piece of cake? A green hard candy? Why do you think so? What other colors do you associate with particular flavors?

❯ Have you ever expected to taste something sweet and discovered it was sour or bitter? What was it? Were you surprised? Why?

After the Exploration

Expected Results

Most investigators will perceive the same flavor that they predict from the gelatin's color, even for the two gelatins with altered colors. Typically, a few investigators will overcome their preconceptions and discern the true flavor of one or both of the altered gelatins.

What's Going On?

The connections we make between the color or appearance of food and its flavor are reinforced on a daily basis; it is rare to encounter a food that does not agree with our expectation of its taste.

When it is possible that at least one of the gelatins may be the flavor its color suggests, you do not know to expect a contradiction; you rely on visual cues, then taste and smell (an intimate part of taste) to determine flavor. Though some of the flavors may be distinct, your expectations of flavor based on color are typically strong enough to influence how you perceive the gelatin's taste.

Discussion Questions

❶ Do you know of any foods that have color added while they are being processed? Why do you think the color is added?

❷ Sometimes a change in the color of food is a sign that the food isn't safe to eat. What are some of these foods and their color changes?

Going Further: Ideas for Inquiry

❯ Examine the ingredient labels on a variety of packaged foods at home or at the market to find out how many have added color.

❯ Conduct a similar activity with foods or drinks that have different flavors but have the same color or are colorless (e.g., flavored, clear mineral waters).

❯ Do people from different cultural backgrounds have the same preconceived notions about relationships between color and flavor? Design and conduct experiments to find out.

The Basics and Beyond

Background

We learn to associate certain colors of foods with particular flavors. Yellow food foretells a lemony flavor; green fruit is likely to be unripe. Because many of these associations are so reliable, we may actually perceive the flavor we expect, rather than the "real" flavor.

Explorer's Guide

Are You a Supertaster?

Find out if your tongue may be extrasensitive to bitter tastes

Do you hate the taste of broccoli or brussels sprouts? If so, it may be because you are especially sensitive to bitter tastes. Do you have broccoli-loving friends? Do you think broccoli tastes the same to them? Examine the surface of your tongue to find a possible connection between the bumps you find there and your sensitivity to bitter flavors.

Things You Will Need

▲ blue food coloring
▲ paper cup
▲ 2 cotton swabs
▲ 2 reinforcement circles for ring-binder paper

▲ magnifying glass
▲ mirror
▲ flashlight
▲ 2 paper towels or napkins
▲ paper for recording data

To Do and Notice

Do this exploration with a partner. You will use the mirror to examine your own tongue while your partner holds the flashlight, or you can have your partner examine your tongue and do the counting. One of you will have your tongue examined first, and then you will trade roles.

❶ Put a few drops of blue food coloring into a paper cup. Dip the tip of a cotton swab into the blue food coloring and use it to paint the tip of your tongue. (You may have your partner do this step, if you wish.) You should cover the first 2 centimeters or so of your tongue with food coloring.

❷ Move your tongue around in your mouth and swallow. This helps to distribute the food coloring evenly.

❸ Lightly pat your tongue dry (once or twice only) with a paper towel or napkin.

❹ Place a notebook paper reinforcement circle on the tip of your tongue, in the position shown in Figure 1.

❺ Have your partner shine a light on this area of your tongue. Use a mirror and a magnifying glass to examine the blue-stained area inside the reinforcement circle.

❻ Look for round, pinkish bumps emerging from the blue background. These are the tops of mushroom-shaped structures on the tongue.

❼ Get a sheet of paper for recording data. Count the number of pink bumps inside the reinforcement circle. There may be many pink bumps crammed together that vary in size, or just a few (see Figure 2). If there are just a few, they may be larger than the ones on someone who has many pink bumps crowded together. If there seem to be too many to count, try to count the number in half the circle and multiply this number by 2. Record the number of pink bumps.

❽ Switch roles and repeat the activity.

Analyzing Data and Drawing Conclusions

How do the number of pinkish bumps on your tongue compare to the number on your partner's tongue? Do either of you dislike certain foods because they taste bitter? Does there seem to be a relationship between the number of pink bumps and a distaste for certain foods?

Displaying Data

If several other pairs of explorers have done this activity as well, collect everyone's data together. Display the data graphically, and use your graph to draw conclusions.

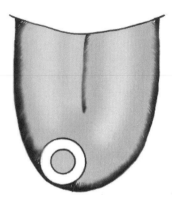

Figure 1:
Placement of the
reinforcement circle

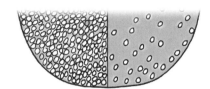

Figure 2: A section of a tongue
showing many bumps
(left) and a section of a
different tongue showing a
few bumps (right)

Facilitator's Guide

Are You a Supertaster?

Materials

for the whole group

▲ blue food coloring

for each pair

▲ paper cup

▲ 2 cotton swabs

▲ 2 reinforcement circles for ring-binder paper

▲ magnifying glass

▲ mirror

▲ flashlight

▲ 2 paper towels or napkins

▲ paper for recording data

Management

▲ Amount of time for the activity: 30 minutes

▲ Preparation time: None, except to gather and distribute materials

▲ Group size: 2

TIP!

● Papillae can be counted indirectly by making a tongue print: Dry the tongue thoroughly, paint it with blue food coloring, then press a piece of white paper firmly onto the painted surface. The fungiform papillae will appear as light or white circles in a field of blue, and can be counted by placing a reinforcement circle on the blue area and counting the white spots.

Preparation and Setup

Activity Overview

Stain the tongue with food coloring, count the number of fungiform papillae within a small circle on the tongue, and relate individual differences in the number of papillae to a sensitivity to bitter tastes.

Concepts

❯ The surface of the tongue is covered with bumps called papillae.

❯ Some of the papillae contain the taste buds that house the taste receptors.

❯ The density of fungiform papillae on the tongue varies from person to person, is probably genetically determined, and may be related to a sensitivity to bitter tastes.

Preparation

None, except for obtaining materials.

Questions for Getting Started

❯ Is the surface of your tongue slick and smooth? Is the surface the same all over your tongue?

❯ There are certain foods that some people like and others hate. What are some of these foods? What do you think accounts for these differences in taste preference?

After the Exploration

Expected Results

A variety of different structures will be seen on the surface of the tongue. The pink bumps that resist taking up the blue food coloring are fungiform papillae. The number of these papillae inside the reinforcement ring will vary from just a few to more than 40.

What's Going On?

Taste research suggests a biological basis for some food preferences and dislikes. Since the fungiform papillae house the taste buds, those individuals with more of these structures will also have more taste buds and a greater likelihood of perceiving some foods as bitter.

❯ A person with more than about 30 fungiform papillae inside the reinforcement circle is probably a "supertaster."

❯ A person with fewer than 10 fungiform papillae inside the ring is probably a "nontaster."

❯ A person with 10 to 30 papillae in the ring is likely a "taster."

Discussion Questions

❶ Were there some foods that you couldn't stand the taste of as a young child, but now enjoy? What do you think caused you to change your taste perceptions?

❷ Do you think that there are other taste perceptions besides bitterness that might be influenced by the number of fungiform papillae that an individual has? Why do you think so?

Going Further: Ideas for Inquiry

❯ Calculate the area in square millimeters inside the reinforcing circle and use this value to express each person's papillae count as a density (number of papillae per square millimeter).

❯ Measure the density of fungiform papillae on different parts of your tongue. Does the density vary with location? What does this suggest about your sense of taste?

❯ If several other pairs of explorers have done this activity, take a poll of the others to see if there is a relationship between the number of papillae in the circle and a tendency to perceive raw broccoli as bitter.

❯ Count the number of papillae of family members. Use this data to construct family trees of "taste" inheritance.

❯ Use another method to assess whether you are a supertaster, a taster, or a nontaster: test your response to a chemical called PROP (see Background for more information). First make PROP testing paper according to the directions on the next page. Then place a piece of the paper in your mouth, moisten it well, and leave it there for a minute or so. If you experience the PROP paper as extremely bitter you are a supertaster; if it tastes somewhat bitter you are a taster; and if you can't discern any bitterness at all you are a nontaster. (Note: PROP is a totally safe chemical. At a dosage of 50 mg per day, it is used to treat hyperthyroidism, but only about 1.6 mg of PROP is present in a piece of PROP paper. You can order pharmaceutical-grade PROP from Pfaltz-Bauer, 172 E. Aurora St., Waterbury, CT 06708, 203-574-0075.)

To make PROP test papers: Heat 500 mL of water to near boiling. Add 5 g of PROP to make a supersaturated solution of PROP. Dip 3-cm circles of Whatman #1 filter paper in the PROP solution so that they are completely soaked. Allow the papers to dry individually on sheets of aluminum foil. Because the PROP solution is supersaturated, the solution will form tiny crystals as it cools. Store the papers individually between sheets of waxed paper.

The Basics and Beyond

Background

The bumps on the surface of the tongue, called papillae, are grouped into three types. The circumvallate papillae are located toward the back of the tongue and form a row like an inverted V. They are several millimeters in diameter and are easily seen in a mirror. The filliform papillae cover the anterior two-thirds of the tongue and are very tiny and conical in shape. They are the most numerous papillae but are not easily seen, even with magnification. The fungiform papillae are shaped like tiny button mushrooms and are the structures that contain the taste buds. They are most densely distributed on the tip of the tongue.

On the surface of the fungiform papillae are taste pores, small openings through which "tastant" molecules enter. Each taste pore leads to a taste bud, which is a cluster of taste receptor cells. When stimulated by tastant molecules, these taste receptors transfer information via nerves to the brain for interpretation. Each fungiform papilla houses between 1 and 15 taste buds.

There is quite a bit of variation in the number of fungiform papillae that people have on their tongues. Taste researchers have discovered that the greater the density of fungiform papillae on the tongue, the greater the likelihood that the individual will be sensitive to bitter tastes. They have divided people into three categories on this basis:

❯ **Supertasters**, who have a high density of fungiform papillae, are especially sensitive to bitter tastes, and generally perceive the taste of raw broccoli, saccharin, unsweetened chocolate, black coffee, and salt substitute (potassium chloride) as extremely bitter.

❯ **Nontasters**, who generally have a low density of fungiform papillae, do not find broccoli and the other foods listed above to be bitter.

❯ **Tasters**, who have a moderate density of papillae, perceive broccoli and the other foods in the list to be bitter, but not intensely so.

Taster status is also determined by the ability to taste certain chemicals. Since the 1930s, scientists have known that people exhibit varying abilities to taste a chemical called PTC (phenylthiocarbamide) and that this ability is genetically inherited. Contemporary taste researchers use a different, more intense chemical called PROP (6-*n*-propylthiouracil) to assess taster status. Supertasters experience paper soaked in PROP as extremely bitter; tasters perceive the same paper as simply bitter; nontasters can't taste the paper at all.

Counting fungiform papillae is very objective—the end result is a number. However, rating the perception of bitterness is a very subjective undertaking that makes taste research particularly challenging. To limit this subjectivity, taste researchers use a device called the "Green Scale" to assess the perception of bitterness. Using the Green Scale, the subject relates the intensity of a taste to the "strongest imaginable sensation" that he or she can imagine. (For more information about the Green Scale, see References.)

References

Green, B. G., G. S. Shaffer, and M. M. Gilmore. A semantically-labeled magnitude scale of oral sensation with apparent ratio properties. *Chemical Senses,* 1993, 18: 683–702.

Bartoshuk, L. M., V. B. Duffy, I. J. Miller. PTC/PROP tasting: Anatomy, psychophysics, and sex effects. *Physiology and Behavior,* 1994, 56: 1165–1171.

Acknowledgments

Our sincere thanks to Dr. Linda Bartoshuk of Yale University School of Medicine for sharing her material, methodology, and research results with us during the development of this activity.

Tidbits

❭ Among those tested so far, about 25% are supertasters, 25% are nontasters, and 50% are tasters.

❭ Almost two-thirds of supertasters are women, and Asians and African-Americans tend to be more sensitive to bitterness than Caucasians.

❭ The ability to taste PTC is a dominant trait that is likely determined by just one gene. Evidence suggests that supertasters are homozygous dominant for the taster gene and that regular tasters are heterozygous.

❭ The cruciferous vegetables, such as broccoli and brussels sprouts, contain bitter chemical compounds called phytochemicals that confer protection from cancer and heart attacks. Even if a supertaster is predisposed to dislike these vegetables, nutritionists recommend preparing them in a manner that makes them more palatable.

❭ It's important to remember that a wide variety of factors, in addition to genetics, can influence one's perception of taste. The quality of the taste stimulus, prior exposure to the stimulus, temperature, age, health, nutritional status, and cultural training all play a role in our perception of taste.

Explorer's Guide

The Nose Knows

Discover the difference between taste and smell

Think of all the wonderful sensations provided by your sense of taste—the sweetness of a perfectly ripe peach, the saltiness of a dill pickle. You can use your sense of taste to tell the difference between two kinds of apples or two kinds of chocolate. How does this power-ful sense actually work? How does your body "taste" things?

Things You Will Need

▲ several different flavors of hard candies (or lollipops)

▲ a stopwatch or clock with a second hand

▲ paper for recording observations

To Do and Notice

Work with a partner in this activity. Choose who will be the first volunteer and who will be the first assistant. You'll reverse roles after you've gone through the activity once.

You may find it helpful to read through the activity and create a data table before you take on the assistant role. You'll be recording the volunteer's experiences and flavor-guesses at three separate times during the activity, and it will be handy to have a prelabeled place to put each observation.

❶ Volunteer: Close your eyes and pinch your nose shut with your fingers.

❷ Assistant: Select a candy, but do not tell the subject the flavor. Unwrap it and place it in the subject's hand. Try not to touch the candy with your fingers.

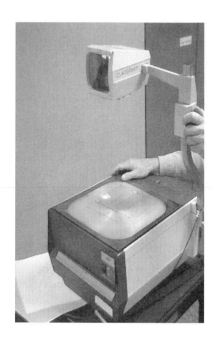

❸ Volunteer: Place the candy in your mouth. Open your eyes—but keep your nose pinched shut! You may breathe through your mouth, but be careful not to inhale the candy into your throat. Focus on the tastes and sensations in your mouth.

❹ Assistant: When the volunteer places the candy in his or her mouth, begin a 60-second countdown. At the same time, ask the volunteer to describe the sensations he or she is experiencing. Quickly record the volunteer's observations in your data table and go to the next step.

❺ Assistant: Ask the volunteer to identify the flavor of the candy. If the volunteer can't do this, record a question mark. If the volunteer is guessing, say so.

❻ Assistant: When the candy has been in the volunteer's mouth for about 60 seconds, again ask the volunteer about the sensations in his or her mouth, and again ask him or her to identify the flavor of the candy. Record both sets of observations.

❼ Assistant: After you've finished recording the information for step 6, tell the volunteer to open his or her nose and immediately describe any differences in the sensations in his or her mouth. Record these observations in your data table, and then ask the volunteer to identify the flavor of the candy.

❽ Assistant: You may now reveal the true flavor of the candy. Record it on the sheet of paper below your data table.

❾ Change roles and repeat the activity.

Interpreting Observations

What sensations did you experience in your mouth? How did these sensations change over time? Could you determine the true flavor of the candy? If so, when? Did your taste sensations change when you opened your nose? What does this tell you about your sense of taste?

Facilitator's Guide
The Nose Knows

Materials

for each small group

▲ several different flavors of individually-wrapped, flavored hard candies (lollipops, which some people find easier to handle, may be used instead)

▲ stopwatch or access to a clock with a second hand

▲ paper for recording observations

Management

▲ Amount of time for the activity: 20–30 minutes

▲ Preparation time: 10 minutes to set out materials

▲ Group size: 2

Preparation and Setup

Activity Overview

Discover the connection between taste and smell by trying to identify the flavors of hard candies through taste alone.

Concepts

❯ There are four tastes that can be recognized by the tongue: sweet, sour, bitter, and salty.

❯ Most of what we experience as taste is actually from our sense of smell.

❯ Particular scents and tastes are due to different molecules that bind to smell and taste receptors.

❯ Our smell receptors can recognize thousands of different scent molecules.

Preparation

None, except for obtaining materials.

Questions for Getting Started

❯ How many different tastes are there? Give examples.

❯ What's the difference between a taste and a particular flavor?

(For example, honey: the taste is sweet; the flavor is honey.)

❯ How does food taste when you have a cold or a stuffy nose?

TIPS!

● To create a common foundation for describing observations in this activity, explain the following definitions before you begin. Taste: one of the four perceptions that come from the tongue's taste receptors—sweet, salty, bitter, and sour. Flavor: a particular kind of taste/smell experience, such as cherry, orange, honey, mint.

● Carry out this activity in concert with the three others that explore the senses of taste and smell, "The Taste of Color," "Are You a Supertaster?" and "Nose-stalgia."

After the Exploration

Expected Results

Subjects are not likely to identify the flavor of the candy when it is first put it in their mouths; they should, however, recognize a sensation of sweetness or sourness or both. After a minute, some subjects may notice that they can identify the flavor. After opening their noses, most subjects can easily identify the flavor, and the sensations in the mouth become more distinct.

What's Going On?

With your nose closed, you are relying on the taste receptors on your tongue alone. Some of these receptors recognize "sweetness" when the hydroxyl groups (-OH) of the sugars in the candy bind to them. Other receptors recognize "sourness" when they come into contact with the hydrogen ions of the acidic compounds in the candy. In a similar way, the ions in salts stimulate "salty" receptors and nitrogen-containing alkaloids stimulate "bitter" receptors. The perceptions of sweetness and sourness provided by the tongue aren't enough to allow you to identify flavors.

After you have sucked on a candy for awhile, you may be able to iden-tify the flavor because the olfactory receptors may begin to come into play. Scent molecules from the candy volatilize and travel into the nasal passages through a "back door"—a passage at the back of the throat. These molecules arrive at the olfactory bulb, a part of the brain that houses the olfactory receptors. The olfactory bulb contains at least 1,000 different types of receptors that allow the average person to distinguish among about 10,000 different scents. The flavor sensations typical of hard candies—cherry, orange, and so on—are produced by specific "flavor" molecules that are recognized by receptors in the olfactory bulb, and not by the tongue's taste receptors.

After you open your nose, the olfactory bulb can do its job unhindered, and sensing the flavor molecules in the candy is relatively easy.

Discussion Questions

❶ Do you think that vision influences your sense of taste? Can you give an example? How would you design an experiment to test your hypothesis?

❷ How do you think culture might influence how people experience the taste and smell of food? What foods might taste good to someone from one cultural background and bad to someone from a different culture?

Going Further: Ideas for Inquiry

❯ Place candies on different areas of your tongue. Do you experience different sensations at the different locations?

❯ Use this activity as the basis of a survey on taste sensitivity. Compare different groups—such as smokers and nonsmokers, or teens and adults—and develop hypotheses to explain any differences between the groups.

The Basics and Beyond

Background

The perception of a food's taste comes from a complex combination of sensory inputs from chemical receptors on the tongue and at the top of the nasal passages. The receptors on the tongue—those responsible for taste per se—are relatively simple: they recognize only sweet, salty, sour, and bitter (and possibly a fifth taste; see Tidbits below). The olfactory (scent) receptors in the nasal passages, in contrast, are fine-tuned and discriminating. They can recognize thousands of different kinds of smells. When we eat food, our brains combine the olfactory receptors' information with the taste information from the tongue to form what we perceive as the food's "taste." When the brain is deprived of smell information (such as when we have colds), food tastes dull because we are only tasting it, not smelling it, too.

Tidbits

❯ Olfactory neurons in the epithelium (outer layer) of the olfactory bulb are the only type of brain cells that are continually and rapidly replaced in adults. Each survives for only about 60 days. These neurons are particularly vulnerable to damage as they are directly exposed to the outside environment. As the cells die, new olfactory neurons are generated by a layer of stem cells underneath the olfactory epithelium.

❯ Alkaloids—the compounds recognized by the tongue's taste sensors as bitter—typically have significant physiological activity. Some examples of alkaloids are nicotine, quinine, morphine, strychnine, and reserpine. Many poisons are alkaloids. Many of the receptors for bitter taste are located at the back of the tongue. This location of the receptors may help to trigger the vomiting response, which could, in theory, prevent poisoning.

❯ Scientists who study taste are debating whether they should recognize the existence of a fifth taste, in addition to sweet, salty, bitter, and sour. This taste is called *umami* and is recognized as "savory," often enhanced by the food additive monosodium glutamate. Most Japanese recognize *umami* as a unique taste and detect it in seaweed, ripe cheeses, and some meats. Interestingly, most non-Japanese do not experience this taste, which suggests that the perception of taste is influenced by culture and language as well as by the functions of the taste and smell sensors.

Explorer's Guide

Nose-stalgia

Explore the power of scent

When you smell fresh-baked chocolate chip cookies, what does the aroma make you think of? Does the scent of Play-doh® or crayons conjure up long-forgotten kindergarten memories? It's common for people to associate certain smells with past experiences or emotions. Explore this connection for yourself.

Things You Will Need

▲ access to 5 "nose-stalgia" cans   ▲ paper for recording observations

To Do and Notice

This activity needs a facilitator to prepare the "nose-stalgia" cans.

Read all the steps below before you begin the activity.

❶ Obtain a "nose-stalgia can" containing a mystery scent. Record the number on the can.

❷ Remove the lid from the can and hold the open can a short distance from your nose. Use your free hand to move the scents released from the can through the air toward your nose. Inhale the scent. If the scent is weak, move the can closer to your nose and try again.

❸ Does the scent make you think of a particular person, place, or situation? Does it evoke any particular feelings or bring to mind any particular memory? Record your observations. If necessary, inhale more of the scent. If you can't connect this scent to a particular memory or emotion, move on to the next step.

❹ Describe the scent that you're exploring. What three adjectives come to mind to describe it? Is it sweet, sour, strong, flowery, spicy, or earthy? Compare the scent to others you know.

❺ Do you recognize the scent? If so, try to name it. If you aren't sure, take a guess or give more than one possibility.

❻ Repeat the process with the remaining nose-stalgia cans. The true names of the scents will be revealed to you when you are done making your observations.

Interpreting Your Observations

Which of the scents evoked a memory or an emotion? Were any of these responses particularly strong or vivid? Did you identify the scents that evoked responses?

Facilitator's Guide
Nose-stalgia

Materials

for the whole group

▲ empty film canisters with lids

▲ cotton balls

▲ 5 strong-scented materials
  (see Preparation)

▲ marking pen for labeling the
  "nose-stalgia cans"

▲ paper for recording observations

Management

▲ Amount of time for the activity:
  20–30 minutes

▲ Preparation time: 20 minutes to
  prepare nose-stalgia cans

▲ Group size: 1

Caution:
Some explorers may have
allergies to certain scents,
so be sure to check with
them or their parents before
conducting the activity.

Preparation and Setup

Activity Overview

Smell a variety of mystery scents, record the impressions each invoke,
and attempt to use olfactory memories to identify each scent.

Concepts

❯ The sense of smell is a chemosense—it involves the detection of
gaseous or volatile molecules.

❯ The nerve impulses triggered by smells go to the brain's centers of
emotion and long-term memory.

Preparation

❶ Obtain 5 strongly scented materials for use in the "nose-stalgia"
cans. Liquid flavor extracts used in cooking, such as vanilla or almond
extract, are ideal. Other good candidates are individual essential oils
(not mixtures), whole herbs or spices such as cinnamon and lavender,
mouthwash, instant sauce mixes, citrus fruit peels, hard candies, flowers
or foliage.

❷ Obtain the other materials. Empty black film cans are readily available at photographic stores.

❸ Make the nose-stalgia cans. For a liquid scent, saturate a cotton ball
with the liquid and place the cotton ball in the film can; then place
another cotton ball over it and replace the lid. For each solid scented
material, place it in the can and cover it with a cotton ball and lid.
In both cases, the top cotton ball helps hide any visual clues to the
identity of the scent. If there are more than a handful of investigators,
it will be helpful to make several identical nose-stalgia cans for
each scent.

❹ Assign each of the scents a unique number and label the cans
accordingly. Keep your own record of what scents are in what cans.

Questions for Getting Started

❯ Why do some things have an odor while other things don't? For example, paper usually doesn't have much of an odor, but a felt marker
does. What characteristics are shared by "smelly" objects that you don't
find in objects without odors?

❯ Does the scent of popping popcorn remind you of any particular experience or person. If so, why do you think so?

❯ How does smell influence taste? Hint: Think about how things smell and taste when you have a head cold.

After the Exploration

Expected Results

Each explorer will typically find some scents to be familiar (even if he or she can't identify them by name) and some scents to be unfamiliar. Some explorers will recall distinct memories or experience certain emotions while inhaling certain scents. Generally, an unfamiliar scent will elicit neither an emotional response nor a memory.

What's Going On?

A familiar scent may elicit memories of times or places associated with that scent because neural impulses carrying information about smell go to the hippocampus, a site of long-term memory storage. Similarly, smells often evoke emotional responses because the smell impulses also go to places within the limbic system (often called the primitive, animal brain).

Discussion Questions

❶ When smelling a scent stimulated a memory or evoked an emotional response, was the scent always one with which you were familiar? What do you think accounts for this observation?

❷ Perfume makers and wine makers need an acute sense of smell to successfully make their products. Do you think the people who work in these professions inherit their acute sense of smell or train their sense of smell? Why?

Going Further: Ideas for Inquiry

❯ Design experiments to test if your memory of other sensory information works like your memory of smells.

❯ Does the sense of smell weaken with age? Conduct explorations to find out.

❯ Choose a scent and determine how low the concentration of that scent can go before you can no longer detect it.

❯ Try to find a particular object (such as a juicy, peeled orange) by your sense of smell alone. Have someone put the object in a room in which all dangerous objects have been removed, then enter the room blindfolded.

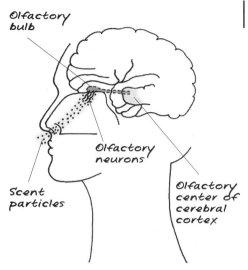

Figure 1: Pathway of scent molecules from nose to brain

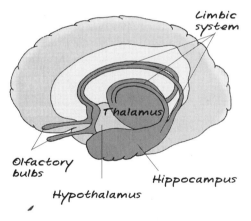

Figure 2: Brain centers involved in the connection between smell and memory

The Basics and Beyond

Background

The sense of smell, also known as olfaction, is a chemosense—a sense that detects the presence of certain chemicals. The other chemosense is taste. In the case of smell, the chemicals that are detected are present in the air, generally as tiny suspended liquid droplets or gaseous molecules.

Odor molecules, or odorants, travel into the nose and up the nasal cavity. At the top of the nasal cavity, they dissolve in mucus covering tissues rich in olfactory receptor neurons. These receptors are of many different types, each with a certain shape that corresponds to the shape of a particular kind of odorant molecule. If an odorant molecule comes into contact with a receptor neuron that matches its shape, it locks on to that receptor site and the neuron then fires.

When an olfactory receptor neuron fires, the impulse is transmitted to the olfactory bulb at the top of the nasal passages, and then shunted in two different directions. One pathway takes the impulse to the olfactory center in the cerebral cortex for perception and recognition of the odor (see Figure 1). The olfactory center is connected to the hypothalamus, which controls maternal and sexual behavior, among other things. The second pathway carries the impulse to the limbic system (see Figure 2), which exerts control over the expression of emotions and instinctive behaviors. One structure within the limbic system, the hippocampus, is intimately involved in the formation and long-term storage of memories.

Scientific evidence suggests that a typical person can discern more than 10,000 different scents, even though there are only about 1000 different types of olfactory receptors. It is believed that each odorant triggers several types of olfactory receptors, creating a unique combination of neural impulses that is interpreted as a single scent.

Tidbits

❯ There are about 10 million olfactory receptor neurons in each of the two nasal cavities.

❯ Through smell, an average human can detect the presence of some molecules at a concentration of less than 1 part in 20 billion, but dogs can detect the presence of certain molecules at a concentration of 1 part in 200 trillion.

❯ After about 30 seconds of exposure to a certain odorant molecule, a human's olfaction system becomes habituated to the odor and rapidly loses the ability to recognize it without a break from that particular stimulus.

❯ Most sensory input travels through the thalamus where it is routed to the appropriate part of the cerebral cortex for interpretation. The olfactory system, however, is an exception—olfactory nerve impulses travel directly to the cortex.

Explorer's Guide

Merry-Go-Round Illusion

*With eyes closed, you
can tell when you are
spinning—but can
you tell when you stop?*

Have you ever had trouble
walking after getting off an
amusement park ride? Even
though you are on solid
ground, it feels like you're
still spinning around. Explore
why this happens.

Things You Will Need

▲ chair or stool that spins quietly   ▲ clock or watch with second hand
▲ paper bag or light-tight blindfold

To Do and Notice

There are two roles in this exploration: rider and observer. The rider spins
around on the chair or stool, and the observer sets the chair or stool spinning and watches the rider. Several people can be observers at the same
time, and you can repeat the exploration so others can be the rider. Read
all the steps before beginning the exploration.

❶ Rider: Sit in the chair or on the stool with your feet slightly off the
ground, not touching the chair. Place the paper bag over your head (or
put the blindfold on) and be sure that you cannot see anything.

❷ Observer: Slowly and steadily rotate the rider in the chair. After about
ten rotations, stop rotating the chair and let the chair spin to a stop.

❸ Rider: Tell the observer when it feels to you that the chair stops moving.

❹ Observer: Take note of the exact moment the chair stops moving and
the exact moment the rider announces the chair has stopped.

Interpreting Your Observations

Was the rider able to accurately judge the time the chair stopped moving?
If not, did the rider's perception of stopped motion come too early or too
late? By how much time? How do you explain these results?

Facilitator's Guide

Merry-Go-Round Illusion

Materials

▲ 1 or more chairs or stools that spin quietly

▲ paper bags or light-tight blindfolds, 1 per chair

▲ clock or watch with second hand

Management

▲ Amount of time for the activity: 10–30 minutes

▲ Preparation time: none

▲ Group size: 2–many, depending on the number of rotating chairs available

> **TIP!**
> ● If only one chair is available, this activity can be done as a demonstration, with one or more volunteers getting spun while others observe.

| Preparation and Setup

Activity Overview

In the absence of visual cues, the semicircular canals in our ears give misleading information.

Concepts

❯ The vestibular system of the inner ear functions to sense movement and help us keep our balance.

❯ When the body or head experiences acceleration, deceleration, or rotation, these movements are sensed by a part of the vestibular system called the semicircular canals.

❯ When the head moves in certain ways, a fluid inside the semicircular canals, called endolymph, also moves, triggering nerve impulses that signal head motion to the brain.

❯ After head motion stops, the endolymph keeps moving for a brief time, signaling continued movement to the brain.

❯ The body often relies on several different sources of sensory cues at once to correctly determine body movement and orientation; when only one source of sensory information is available, it can be interpreted erroneously.

Preparation

None, except for obtaining the materials.

Questions for Getting Started

❯ What sensations do you experience when you spin around and around and then suddenly stop?

❯ When you close your eyes on a roller coaster or other ride, how do you know you are moving?

After the Exploration

Expected Results

If the room and chair are sufficiently quiet and the bag cuts off vision completely, most riders who spin in the chair will misjudge the end of their rotation by one to several seconds.

What's Going On?

As the chair rotates, the endolymph in the rider's semicircular canals (the one in each ear that is parallel to the ground) moves through the canal and over a bulge at the main body of the inner ear. The endolymph bends hair cells in this bulge. As a result, nerves at the base of the hair cells fire nerve impulses to the brain at an increased rate. This acceleration in the rate of firing is interpreted by the brain as rotation.

After the rotation of the chair stops, there is a short delay in the movement of the endolymph back to its normal position. During this short lag period, nerve impulses are still telling the brain that the body is rotating, even though it isn't. Without visual cues to contradict this information, the rider perceives that he or she is still moving.

Discussion Questions

❶ Ear infections sometimes affect people's sense of balance. Why do you think this occurs?

❷ Close your eyes and walk a straight line. How do you keep your balance without vision?

❸ Why is it useful for an organism (such as yourself) to be able to know it is rotating, even when it can't see?

Going Further: Ideas for Inquiry

❯ Spin around rapidly several times, stop suddenly, and then either try to walk a straight line or point to a person right in front of you. Develop a scientific explanation for the results of this exploration.

❯ How do astronauts perceive motion? Research how the perception of motion is affected by being in free fall.

❯ Demonstrate what happens to the fluid in the inner ear with a simple model. Fill a cup part way with water and sprinkle some coarse pepper or similar substance on the surface of the water. Rotate the cup to simulate a rotating person. Watch as the pepper flecks also begin to rotate like the endolymph in the inner ear. Then stop rotating the cup and note how the pepper flecks continue to rotate. How does this simulate what happens in your inner ear? Can you design other models to illustrate the same phenomenon?

The Basics and Beyond

Background

The vestibular system in the inner ear provides our brains with important information about the movement and orientation of our bodies. Part of this system, the semicircular canals, functions to sense rotational movements in any plane. A fluid inside the arched canals, called endolymph, moves in response to rotational movements such as falling and spinning, and in so doing bends hairs inside the canals. The movement of the hairs triggers nerve impulses that the brain interprets as movement. Normally we rely both on visual cues and the information from the semicircular canals to correctly interpret our movement; when deprived of visual cues, the semicircular canals alone can provide misleading information.

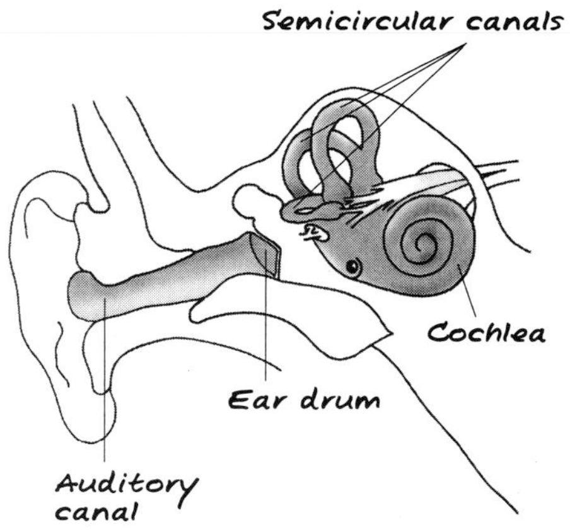

Figure 1: Structure of the human ear

Tidbits

❯ There are three semicircular canals in each ear, each occupying a different plane in space. One detects movement in a plane parallel to the ground, and the other two detect movement in planes perpendicular to the ground but at right angles to each other.

❯ Physicians only use water at body temperature to flush out ears. If cold water is used, it will set up convection currents in the endolymph, triggering extreme nausea.

❯ We have rocks in our heads! In addition to the semicircular canals, the vestibular system has organs, the utricle and saccule, that contain crystals of calcium carbonate (limestone). Called otoliths, these crystals move within a gelatinous membrane, triggering nerve impulses from hair cells similar to those in the semicircular canals. The otolith organs detect the head's position relative to the downward pull of gravity, as well as linear acceleration and deceleration.

Explorer's Guide

Do You Know Where Your Hands Are?

How do you know what your arms, legs, and body are doing without looking?

Can you put a bite of food in your mouth with your eyes closed? Sure you can! But how do you know where your arms and hands are when you can't see them? Some experiments will help you figure out how this works.

Things You Will Need

▲ lined paper   ▲ pencil

To Do and Notice

Finding Your Fingers

You'll be trying to touch each of your 10 fingertips with your eyes closed. Before you begin, read steps 1–5 below to see how you will do this, and then predict how many times out of ten you'll be successful. Record this prediction.

It's very important in this activity for you to keep your eyes closed the entire time, work quickly, and carefully observe how your body responds.

❶ Close your eyes and raise both hands above your head. Keep the fingers of your left hand totally still (no wiggling!).

❷ Touch the tip of your right index finger to the tip of your nose, then quickly use the same finger to try to touch the tip of your left thumb. Keep your left hand still. Even if you "miss," go on quickly to the next step.

❸ Again touch the tip of your nose with your right index finger and immediately use the same finger to try to touch the tip of your left index finger.

❹ Repeat the process three more times, each time trying to touch a different finger on your left hand. Keep track of how many times you succeed in touching the correct finger, and record your observations.

❺ Switch hands: hold your right hand still in the air above your head and use your left index finger to touch your nose, your right thumb, your nose, your right index finger, your nose, and so on. Record your observations.

How successful were you at finding each fingertip? Does your performance improve with time? Is there a difference between your two hands?

❻ Now repeat the activity, but this time slightly wiggle the fingers of the hand you hold in the air. Are you more successful this time? If so, can you think of a reason why?

Finding the X

Before doing the activity, read all of these directions and then predict how many tries it will take you to hit the "X" with your eyes closed.

❶ Mark an X about 1 cm tall on a piece of paper. Observe its position on the paper.

❷ Grasp your pencil and close your eyes. Raise the pencil above your head and then lower it to the paper, trying to make a dot as near as possible to the X.

❸ Open your eyes and check your results. If your dot was not directly on the X, repeat step 2 until you hit the X or until you've tried about six times.

❹ Record your observations.

Did you hit the X on the first attempt? How close were you to your predicted number of attempts?

Writing Without Looking

❶ On a lined sheet of paper, write your name.

❷ Place your pencil on the line just below your name, close your eyes, and write your name again.

❸ Compare the two written names. Is there much difference in their appearance? Record your results and observations.

Interpreting Your Observations

What generalizations can you make about your ability to do things with your hands without using your sense of vision?

Facilitator's Guide

Do You Know Where Your Hands Are?

Materials

for each investigator

▲ lined paper

▲ pencil

Management

▲ Amount of time for the activity: 20–30 minutes

▲ Preparation time: none

▲ Group size: 1

Preparation and Setup

Activity Overview

Perform simple tasks that require sensing the position of the hands and fingers in space without the benefit of vision, and use the experiences to learn how proprioceptors provide information about the position of the body and its appendages.

Concepts

❯ Proprioceptors, also known as stretch receptors, are tiny sensors in muscles, tendons, joints, and ligaments that detect tension, elongation, and other changes.

❯ Proprioception provides us with an unconscious assessment of body position and posture.

❯ While proprioception provides us with a general sense of the position of our body's appendages, most of us rely on vision for more detailed information.

Preparation

None.

Questions for Getting Started

❯ Where are your feet right now? Are your legs crossed or not? How do you know?

❯ Do you think you could brush your teeth in complete darkness? How would you find your mouth if you couldn't see it?

TIPS!

● The first exploration, *Finding Your Fingers,* captures the essence of proprioception. Therefore, the other two can be skipped if time is short.

● It may be helpful to demonstrate the *Finding Your Fingers* activity.

After the Exploration

Expected Results

❯ In *Finding Your Fingers,* explorers generally are surprised that they have such a difficult time accurately touching their fingertips. Their success usually improves when they wiggle the fingers of the target hand.

❯ In *Finding the X,* explorers usually notice that their performance improves with repeated trials; they may notice in particular the importance of concentrating visually on the position of the X between trials.

❯ In *Writing Without Looking,* most explorers find it surprisingly easy to write legibly with their eyes closed, especially in light of the difficulties encountered in the first two activities.

What's Going On?

Proprioceptors in the muscles, tendons, ligaments, and joints are used to judge body positions in all of these activities. Since most of us are highly dependent on visual cues for judging distances and positions, proprioception alone is not enough to give our brains the detailed information needed to complete these activities with great accuracy.

In *Finding Your Fingers,* the wiggling of the fingers in the target hand increases the success rate because it causes elongations, contractions, and tension changes in that hand, which are detected by the proprioceptors there. With this information, the brain is better able to picture the location of the target hand in space.

In *Finding the X,* performance usually improves with several trials because, over time, the brain gets better at integrating the visual information it receives prior to relying on proprioception alone.

In *Writing Without Looking,* it is relatively easy to write "blindly" because the proprioceptors in our hands and fingers are very "experienced" in providing positional information while we write and can compensate for the lack of visual information.

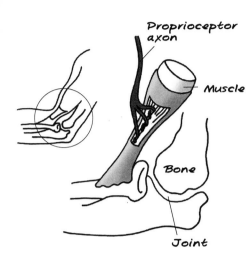

Figure 1:
A proprioceptor in
a human arm

Discussion Questions

❶ How can you form letters and write across a straight line when you can't see?

❷ Predict some of the things that might happen if you lost your sense of proprioception.

❸ How do you think visually impaired people can navigate through the world even though they cannot see well or can't see at all?

Going Further: Ideas for Inquiry

❭ Is a person's dominant hand better at performing the tasks in this exploration than his or her other hand? Form a hypothesis and test it.

❭ Test how practice affects the success rate in *Finding Your Fingers*. Have some friends do the activity wiggling their fingers the first time and keeping them still the second. Then compare these results to what you observed the first time you did the activity (when the wiggling came second).

❭ Create your own ways of further investigating proprioception.

❭ Invite a visually impaired person to come and talk about how he or she experiences his or her body in space.

The Basics and Beyond

Background

Even with your eyes closed, you have a sense of body position—where your arms and legs are; whether your back is straight, hunched, or arched; how you are holding your head. This sense of body position comes from information sent to your brain by proprioceptors, tiny sensors in your muscles, tendons, joints, and inner ear. The proprioceptors detect stretching, elongation, and other changes; this information is used by your brain to create an unconscious picture of the body and its parts in three-dimensional space.

Sighted people normally use visual information more than proprioception to perform tasks that require precise judgment of body position. When people have to perform such tasks without benefit of their sense of sight, they are forced to rely on proprioception alone, and this experience allows them to explore this taken-for-granted "sixth" sense.

Explorer's Guide

aMAZE-ing Memories

With tactile input from your finger, you can create a good mental map of a maze

In your own home, can you find your way to the bathroom at night in total darkness? What about at a friend's house? Find out how your sense of touch can help you remember how to move around in the world.

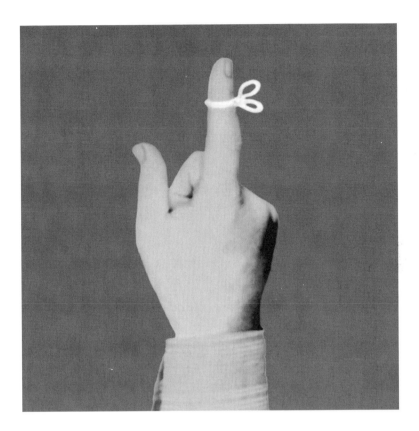

Things You Will Need

▲ a finger maze in a brown paper grocery bag

▲ stopwatch or access to clock with second hand

▲ paper for recording data

To Do and Notice

This activity works best with a facilitator.

The maze inside the paper bag is a finger maze. It has raised lines that you can follow with your finger, using just your sense of touch.

Work with a partner to do this activity. One person runs the maze twice in a row, while the other person times how long it takes and records the times. Then you switch roles so the other person can run the maze.

Don't peek at the maze until the activity is completed or you'll spoil the fun!

❶ Place your hand just inside the paper bag. Touch the maze with your index finger and find the triangle shape, which is the starting point for the maze.

❷ When your partner says "go," begin running the maze. Use your index finger only to follow the raised line until you reach the end of the maze, which is a circle shape. You may encounter "dead ends" in the maze—paths that lead nowhere.

❸ When you find the circle, say "stop." Your partner will record your time.

❹ Immediately run the maze again while your partner times the process and records your time for this second run.

❺ Switch roles.

❻ After you've both run the maze twice, take it out of the bag to look at it.

Analyzing Data and Drawing Conclusions

Did you complete the maze any faster the second time through? If so, how do you explain your improved performance?

Facilitator's Guide
aMAZE-ing Memories

Materials

for the whole group

▲ cardstock or old manila folders

▲ glitter glue or structural paint (available at art stores)

for each pair

▲ a finger maze in a brown paper grocery bag

▲ stopwatch or access to clock with second hand

▲ paper for recording data

Management

▲ Amount of time for the activity: 20–30 minutes

▲ Preparation time: 1 hour to make a set of mazes

▲ Group size: 2

Preparation and Setup

Activity Overview

Without benefit of vision, run simple finger mazes and discover that the brain can memorize tactile sensations and use them to create a mental map.

Concepts

❯ We use our sense of touch to navigate through the world, especially when we cannot see our surroundings.

❯ Activities become easier with experience because of the brain's ability to remember what the activities involve.

❯ The formation of memories is a complex process that involves all of our senses.

Preparation

❶ Make the finger mazes. For each maze, draw a pattern on cardstock or an old manila folder, large enough to cover much of the surface. Use the patterns on pages 145–146, or make up your own similar patterns. Each maze must have a triangle as a starting point and a circle as an ending point; it should also have at least one dead end. Apply glitter glue or structural paint to the pattern to form a raised line. Let the glue or paint dry overnight.

❷ Place each maze in a brown paper bag with the starting point (triangle) toward the front of the bag. Secure each maze in its bag with a few small pieces of tape.

Questions for Getting Started

❯ Have you ever tried to find your way in a very dark room? How did you do it?

❯ Do you remember how you learned to ride a bike (shoot baskets, hit a baseball, roller skate, etc.)? Did it get easier with time?

After the Exploration

Expected Results

The time it takes to run the finger mazes will vary considerably among different people, depending on the difficulty of the maze and the skill of the person. In most cases, however, the maze will be completed much more quickly the second time.

What's Going On?

When you run a maze the first time, you use only your sense of touch to navigate to the end of the maze. In the process you create a mental map of some of the maze's pattern and "store" the map in your short-term memory. The map helps you avoid dead ends on the second run-through, and allows you to complete the maze more quickly.

Discussion Questions

❶ How important is the sense of touch to someone with impaired vision? Why?

❷ Do all your memories stay with you for life? Do you think you'll remember the pattern of your maze tomorrow? Next month?

❸ How do our other senses help us to form memories?

Going Further: Ideas for Inquiry

❯ After you complete the maze the second time, and before you look at it, try drawing it on paper. Then compare your drawing to the actual maze.

❯ Create your own finger mazes to use with family members and friends.

❯ Repeat the activity with your nondominant hand and a different maze. Compare your results to what you recorded with your dominant hand.

The Basics and Beyond

Background

The brain has the ability to encode amazingly precise memories of sensory experiences, whether they are visual, auditory, olfactory, tactile, or taste-related. We can draw on these memories if we need to in the process of solving physical problems or completing unfamiliar activities.

For sighted people, it's not normally important to remember tactile experiences in any precise way. But when the sense of sight isn't available, tactile experiences can be remembered surprisingly well.

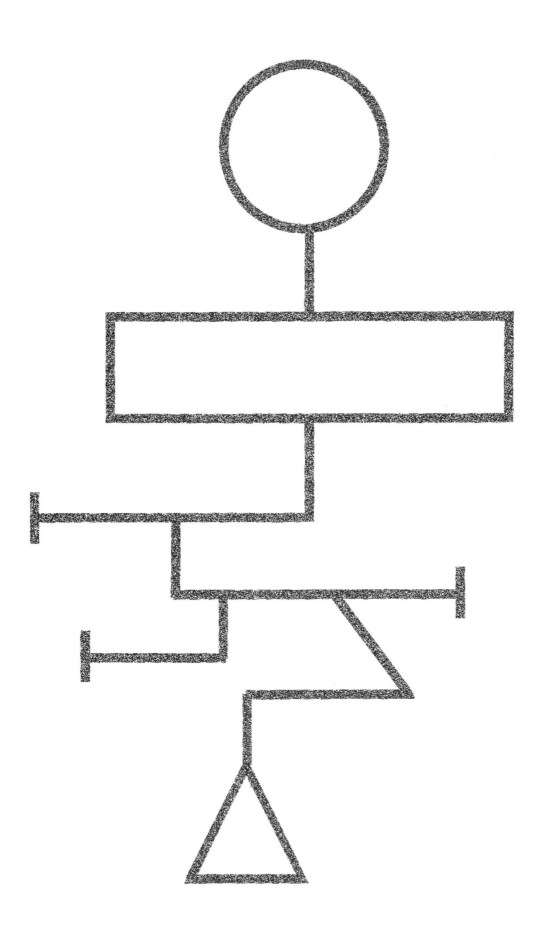

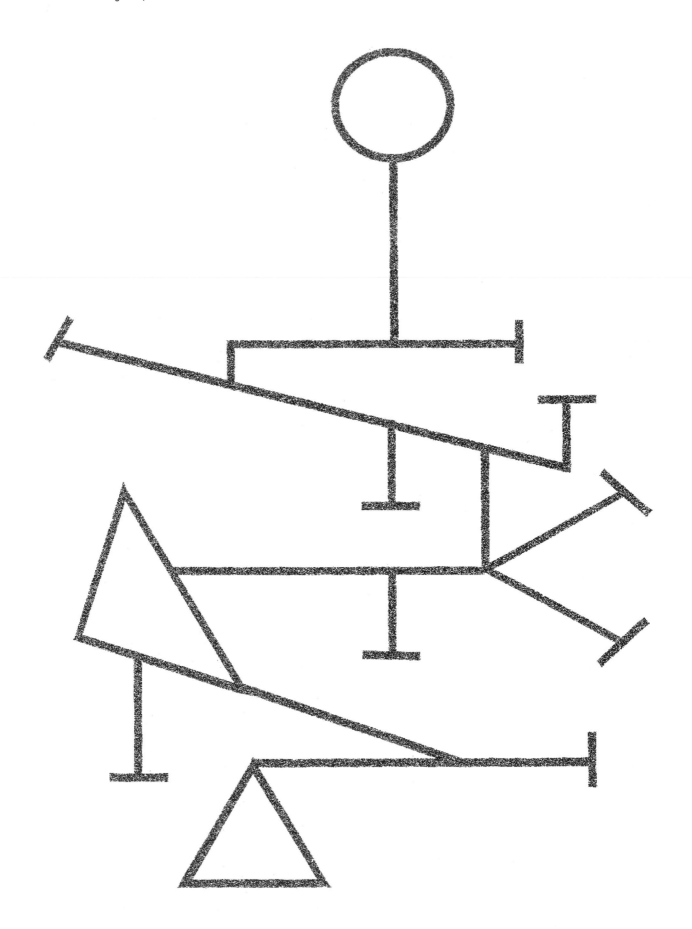

Explorer's Guide

Riddle of the Sphincter

How fast does water travel from your mouth to your stomach?

Do you think that you could swallow water while standing on your head? How do astronauts swallow their dinner while they are in free-fall conditions in the space shuttle? Why don't you see your lunch again if you stand on your head right after eating? Conduct some experiments to find out!

Things You Will Need

▲ 2 paper cups, marked with a line at 40 mL
▲ stopwatch, or clock with second hand
▲ meterstick or tape measure
▲ stethoscope
▲ cotton balls and small cup of disinfectant
▲ 2 straws (optional)
▲ access to a large mirror
▲ access to a pitcher of water
▲ paper for recording data

To Do and Notice

Do this activity with a partner. The room must stay quiet because you'll be listening for very soft sounds inside your body.

Hearing your gastroesophageal valve

❶ Stand in front of a mirror and swallow water. Feel the movements of your tongue and watch the movements of your larynx (Adam's apple) in the mirror.

❷ Clean the earpieces of a stethoscope with disinfectant.

❸ Listen to your heartbeat with the stethoscope. If you can hear your heartbeat clearly, you are using the stethoscope correctly. Let your partner hear his or her heartbeat. Remember to clean the earpieces each time the other person uses the stethoscope.

❹ Decide if you or your partner will go first. Fill your cup to the line with water.

❺ Position the disk end of the stethoscope on your abdomen slightly to the left of, and just below the end of, your sternum, or breastbone. With the stethoscope in this location (shown in Figure 1), you will be able to hear the sounds made by your gastroesophageal sphincter, a ring of tissue at the top of your stomach. This structure acts like a valve, allowing food to enter, but not easily exit, your stomach.

❻ Sip all of the water from the cup without swallowing. Now swallow the water, and listen for a gurgling sound in the stethoscope a few seconds after you swallow. The gurgling sound is the water trickling through your gastroesophageal sphincter into your stomach.

❼ If you didn't hear a gurgling sound, try repeating step 6. If you still don't hear the sound, shift the position of the disc slightly and repeat step 6 again. If you have trouble hearing your own valve, try listening to your partner's abdomen while he or she swallows water.

❽ Disinfect the earpieces on the stethoscope. Switch places so that your partner can hear his or her gastro-esophageal valve.

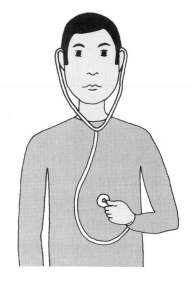

Figure 1: Placement
of stethoscope

Timing a gulp of water from mouth to stomach

❶ Measure the distance in centimeters from your mouth to the top of your stomach (at the base of your sternum). Record this distance.

❷ Predict how long it will take water to travel from your mouth to your stomach, and record this prediction.

Now, one of you will swallow water and listen for the sound of your valve. The other will work the stopwatch.

❸ Fill your cup to the line with water. Position the stethoscope as before. Sip all of the water, but do not swallow it yet. When you begin to swallow, signal your partner to begin timing.

❹ Signal your partner again as soon as you start to hear gurgling from your gastroesophageal valve. Your partner will stop timing at your signal. Record the number of seconds between swallow and gurgle.

❺ Change roles. Disinfect the earpieces. Repeat steps 3 and 4.

❻ Do the experiment two more times, so that each of you completes three trials.

❼ Calculate and record the average of your three trials. Then, divide the distance the water traveled by the average time in seconds it took to travel that distance. This figure is the rate of movement of the water through your esophagus. Record this rate in units of centimeters per second (cm/s).

Investigating the role of gravity

❶ Predict how long it will take water to travel from your mouth to your stomach when you are lying down and when you are sitting with your head between your knees.

❷ Test your predictions. Repeat the experiment as before, doing three trials while lying down and three more while sitting with your head between your knees. (You can do it one way and your partner the other.) In each of these positions, it may be easiest to sip the water with a straw. Record your results, and calculate an average time and a rate of movement for each position.

Analyzing Data and Drawing Conclusions

Does the rate of movement of water in the esophagus vary between the three positions? If so, how? What do your data suggest about the role of gravity in transporting materials from your mouth to your stomach?

Student	Standing Rate	Standing Ave	Lying Down Rate	Lying Down Ave	Sitting Rate	Sitting Ave
1	15.15	3.3	15.15	3.3	—	—
2	6.2	5	14.5	2	9.5	3.3
3	10.9	3.5	11.4	3½	—	
4	5.25	2.7	3	4.7	2.5	5.7
5	5.25	2.7	3	4.7	2.5	5.7
6	4.7	7	4.71	7	3.75	8.8
7	5.08	6½	4.58	7.2	3.66	9
8	13.3	2.7	6.3	5.7	4.73	7.6
9	11	3	6	5.5	5	7
10	13.3	2.33	9.3	3.33	10⅓	3
11	11.985	2.67	8.72	3.67	5.33	6
12	9.5	4	6.7	5⅔	7.12	5⅓
13	6	6	—	—	—	—
14	15.2	2.3	9.86	3.66	6.56	5.33
15	10.58	2.6	6.75	4	13.5	2
16	4.57	7	4	8	3.2	10
17	6.2	5	14.5	2	9.39	3.7
18	4.31	7.2	5.2	6	3.72	8.3
19	15	2.7	4	6	6.7	5⅓
20	12.03	2.66	7.6	7.33	5.33	6
21	13.9	2.3	9.6	3.33	10.4	3
22	9.2	3.33	9.56	3.66	6.3	6.6

Facilitator's Guide

Riddle of the Sphincter

Materials

for the whole group

▲ 1 or 2 large mirrors (for observing swallowing)

▲ several pitchers of water distributed around the room

for each pair

▲ 2 paper cups, marked with a line at 40 mL

▲ stopwatch, or clock with second hand

▲ meterstick or tape measure

▲ stethoscope

▲ cotton balls and small cup of rubbing alcohol or other disinfectant

▲ 2 straws (optional)

▲ paper for recording data

Management

▲ Amount of time for the activity: 45 minutes

▲ Preparation time: 15 minutes to distribute materials

▲ Group size: 2

Preparation and Setup

Activity Overview

Learn about the role of peristalsis in getting food or fluid from the mouth to the stomach by measuring the length of time it takes water to travel between these two locations.

Concepts

❯ Movements of the mouth, tongue, and larynx are involved in swallowing.

❯ Swallowed material travels from the mouth to the pharynx (throat) to the esophagus, and then through the gastroesophageal sphincter into the stomach.

❯ Involuntary muscular contractions in the esophagus propel food and fluid to the stomach independent of gravity.

❯ The involuntary muscular contractions of the esophagus and other parts of the digestive tract are called peristalsis.

Preparation

❶ Obtain the necessary materials. Inexpensive stethoscopes can be purchased from many pharmacies.

❷ Mark each paper cup with a line at 40 mL.

Questions for Getting Started

❯ Can you trace the path of food through the entire digestive tract? What are all the internal organs that are involved in swallowing and digestion?

❯ Have you ever tried to swallow food or drink while standing on your head? What do you think would happen if you tried to do this?

TIPS!

● Practice using the stethoscopes prior to doing the activity.

● Emphasize the need for quiet during the activity.

After the Exploration

Expected Results

The rate of movement of water through the esophagus should vary little among the three different positions.

What's Going On?

The muscular movements of peristalsis move water or food through the esophagus independent of the force of gravity. Therefore, no matter what the position of the body, the rate of movement of material through the esophagus is a function of the rate of peristaltic contractions.

Fluid or food moves through the gastroesophageal sphincter into the stomach only when squeezed through by peristaltic action. Water moving through the sphincter causes the gurgling sound heard through the stethoscope. Without the gastroesophageal sphincter, the pressure of the diaphragm on the stomach during each exhalation of breath would cause the stomach contents to move backwards into the esophagus, creating unpleasant burning sensations. Some people have this problem, which is called acid reflux. When you vomit, the muscular contractions of your stomach are so strong that your stomach contents are easily ejected through the sphincter.

Discussion Questions

❶ Compare the results for the tallest and shortest explorers. Why is it important to compare the rate of movement from person to person, rather than just the time it took for water to reach the stomach?

❷ What are some of the challenges astronauts face while eating in "weightless" situations? Do you think that they have trouble swallowing food or water?

Going Further: Ideas for Inquiry

❯ Use the stethoscope to listen to what's happening in your stomach. Try to figure out the causes of the sounds you hear.

❯ Try listening to your stomach and your intestines with a stethoscope at different hours after you've eaten. Can you follow the path of food through your digestive tract? Do you hear particular sounds at certain times after eating? What do you think causes all the different sounds?

The Basics and Beyond

Background

When you swallow, your tongue moves up and back, pushing food and water into the pharynx. As this occurs, the larynx bobs up, moving the epiglottis, a flap of tissue, to a position atop the pharynx, where it blocks the opening to the trachea. By blocking the trachea, the epiglottis prevents water and food from being inhaled into the lungs during swallowing.

The swallowed material moves from the pharynx into the "food tube," or esophagus. Then the swallowed material is propelled through the esophagus by cycles of contraction and relaxation of muscles lining the esophageal walls. These movements are called peristalsis. Peristalsis allows food and fluid to move through the esophagus regardless of its orientation to the force of gravity.

When swallowed material approaches your stomach, peristalsis forces it through the gastroesophageal sphincter, a circular band of muscle located at the upper end of the stomach, just below the sternum. The function of this sphincter is to prevent food from flowing backward from the stomach into the esophagus. Water moving through this sphincter causes a gurgling sound, which you can hear with a stethoscope.

Tidbits

❯ The gastroesophageal sphincter in some animals (such as rodents) is so strong that they can't vomit. This works to the animals' disadvantage when they eat poisons put out by humans. They can't get rid of the poison and it kills them.

❯ The small intestine moves food along by peristalsis, just like the esophagus, but it also squeezes the intestinal contents forward and backward to mix them with digestive juices and press them against the intestinal wall for absorption of nutrients. This forward-and-backward movement is called segmentation.

❯ When stomachs growl, they are contracting around air. The contractions and growling sound they make are called borborygmous (from the Greek word for "rumbling").

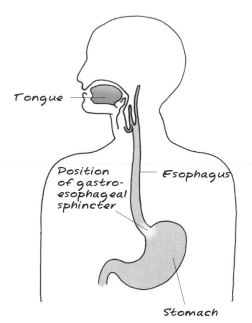

Figure 2: Digestive pathway from mouth to stomach

Explorer's Guide

Sweaty Fingers

Your body sometimes does things without your permission

How do you feel when you have to give a presentation in front of a group of people at school or work? Do you get a bit nervous? Does your stomach tighten a bit and do the palms of your hands sweat? Take a close look at the sweat pores on your fingertips and find out what else besides presentations can make you sweat.

Things You Will Need

▲ a dissecting microscope (or hand-held 30× magnifier)

▲ ice, warm water, feather (all optional)

▲ paper for recording observations

To Do and Notice

Observing

❶ Place the tip of one index finger, palm side up, on the stage of your microscope. Focus on the skin of your fingertip with the low power of the microscope.

❷ Notice the ridges and valleys on your fingertip. These are what make up your fingerprint.

❸ Without moving the index finger you are viewing, increase the magnification of the microscope to the higher power (30×). Refocus on your fingertip as needed.

❹ The ridges and valleys of your fingerprints now appear much larger. Notice that in the "valleys" there are small, shadowy depressions. You may have to adjust the focus, the light, or both to see these depressions. They are the pores of your sweat glands.

You may see something coming out of the pores. This is sweat! If you don't see the pores at first, seeing the sweat that comes out of them may help you find them. When you are sure that you can identify your sweat pores, move on to the next part of the exploration.

Experimenting

Try to discover what can increase the rate at which sweat comes out of the pores.

❶ Leave one hand under the microscope or magnifier so that you can observe the pores on one fingertip.

❷ Lightly bite a finger on your free hand—hard enough to cause some pain but no damage. Carefully observe your pores to see if there is any change in the rate of sweat production. Record your observations.

❸ Think of other kinds of stimuli that may cause you to sweat more. Test the effect of each one by watching your sweat pores through the microscope while you "apply" the stimulus. Here are some ideas: Place your free hand in hot (but not too hot!) water; hold on to an ice cube; have someone tickle you with a feather; have someone startle you; watch the scary part of a movie on videotape.

Interpreting Your Observations

For which stimuli did you notice an increase in the rate of sweat production on your fingertip? Do these stimuli have anything in common? What do your observations suggest about sweating as a response to certain situations?

Facilitator's Guide
Sweaty Fingers

Materials

for each pair or small group

▲ dissecting (stereo) microscope or hand-held 30× magnifier

▲ ice, warm water, feathers (all optional)

▲ paper for recording observations

Management

▲ Amount of time for the activity: 30 minutes

▲ Preparation time: none

▲ Group size: 1–3 or more, depending on availability of microscopes or magnifiers

Preparation and Setup

Activity Overview

A microscope reveals fingertip sweat pores. The relationship between various stimuli and rate of sweating can be investigated.

Concepts

❯ Sweating is one of the most important ways in which the body regulates its internal temperature.

❯ Increased rates of sweating are part of the body's "fight or flight" response to stress, which is controlled by the autonomic nervous system.

Preparation

None, except for obtaining materials.

Questions for Getting Started

❯ What do you feel happening in your body when you are startled by sudden loud sounds?

❯ Do you blush when you're embarrassed? Do you have any physical control over this response?

After the Exploration

Expected Results

The sweat glands in the skin of the fingertips constantly produce a small amount of sweat, even under relaxed conditions. Most explorers will be able to observe this sweat coming out of their pores.

All the stimuli suggested should cause an observable increase in the rate of sweating. Observant investigators may note that after they are exposed to a particular stimulus repeatedly or for a long period of time, they no longer sweat at an increased rate.

TIP!
● Demonstrate what the sweat-gland openings look like with a video microscope.

What's Going On?

The small amount of sweat production observed initially is part of the body's normal and relatively constant processes of temperature regulation and waste expulsion. The increased rate of sweat production observed after exposure to the various stimuli is part of the body's "fight or flight" response, which is controlled by a part of the autonomic nervous system called the sympathetic division.

When we are excited or find ourselves in threatening or stressful situations, the sympathetic division causes the adrenal glands to secrete epinephrine and norepinephrine, hormones that quickly produce a number of changes in the body, including increases in heart rate, blood pressure, and blood glucose levels, and dilation of the blood vessels in the skeletal muscles and the lung bronchioles. Many other events—such as increased sweating—also occur. These changes prepare the body for responding to a threat, and they remain until the hormones are broken down in the liver.

Emotional upset and even minor physical stress can stimulate the sympathetic nervous system and kick in a short-lived "fight or flight" response. The stimuli suggested in this activity generally cause this kind of minor response and increase the rate of sweating, which can be observed on the sweat pores of the fingertips.

Discussion Questions

❶ How do you think antiperspirants work?

❷ You often sweat when you have a fever. Why do you think this happens?

Going Further: Ideas for Inquiry

❯ Examine the labels of several antiperspirants. What are the active ingredients? Research how they work.

❯ Apply an antiperspirant to your fingertip. Does it prevent or reduce the production of fingertip sweat? Do some brands work better than others in reducing perspiration?

The Basics and Beyond

Background

The skin over most areas of the human body is covered with eccrine sweat glands. These glands produce what we commonly call "sweat," which is made up of water plus salts, traces of metabolic wastes, and vitamin C. The ducts of these glands open externally as funnel-shaped pores.

The eccrine sweat glands are an important and efficient part of the body's heat regulation system. Nerve endings in the glands cause them to secrete sweat when the external temperature or body temperature is high. As sweat evaporates, it cools the body.

The eccrine sweat glands may also produce sweat in response to a variety of stimuli, including pain, fear, and stress. These responses are controlled involuntarily by the body's autonomic nervous system.

Tidbits

❯ The axillary (armpit) and genital areas of the body have an additional kind of sweat gland, called apocrine glands. Apocrine glands are larger than eccrine glands; their secretions, in addition to the elements in regular sweat, contain fatty acids and proteins. The duct of each apocrine gland empties onto a hair follicle.

❯ The average human body is covered with approximately 2.5 million sweat glands.

❯ Facial "pores" are not the same as eccrine sweat gland pores; what we see on the face are actually the external outlets of hair follicles.

❯ Sweat is acidic (pH 4–6); this acidity inhibits the growth of bacteria that are always present on the skin.

❯ On a hot day, it is possible to lose up to 7 liters of body water through sweating.

❯ If the internal body temperature deviates more than a few degrees from the normal 98.6°F, potentially life-threatening changes begin to occur in the body. Sweating helps to prevent over-heating of the body when the environment is too hot.

Explorer's Guide
Circle of Nerves

How long does it take you to respond to a stimulus?

You're a sprinter set in the starting blocks, waiting to run the 100-meter dash. A quick start is critical. How long do you think it will take you to tell your muscles to launch your body out of the blocks after you hear the starting gun? Participate in an activity that will help you answer a similar question.

Things You Will Need

▲ stopwatch
▲ paper for recording data

▲ chalkboard and chalk, or equivalent

To Do and Notice

You'll need a minimum of about eight people to do this activity. A larger number is fine.

Be sure to read all the steps below before you begin.

❶ Form a large circle with all explorers facing the inside. One person should volunteer for the critical job of "timer." The timer stands outside the circle.

❷ Decide which person in the circle will be the "starter."

❸ Hold hands in the circle and close your eyes.

❹ The starter will start the activity by squeezing the left hand of the person to his or her right. As soon as that person to the right feels the squeeze, he or she squeezes the left hand of the next person in the circle, and so on around the circle until the "impulse" returns to the starter.

❺ To time the process, the starter shouts "go" at exactly the same time that he or she squeezes the hand of the person to the right. The timer begins timing with the stopwatch when he or she hears the "go." When the impulse goes all the way around the circle and returns to the starter, the starter says "stop!" and the timer stops timing. Then the time it took for the impulse to go around the circle is recorded by the timer where everyone can see it.

❻ Practice this activity at least once before recording the results. It can take the group a few practice rounds to get the hang of it. When the group feels ready, conduct the activity three times, each time recording the number of seconds it takes for the impulse to travel around the circle.

Analyzing Data and Drawing Conclusions

Find the average of the three times. Divide this average time by the number of people in the circle. The result is the average time it took for each person's nervous system to process the stimulus of the hand squeeze in the left hand and tell the muscles of the right hand to squeeze in response. What does this length of time tell you about how your nervous system works? What parts of the brain and nervous system are involved in this exploration?

Facilitator's Guide
Circle of Nerves

Materials

▲ stopwatch

▲ chalkboard and chalk, or equivalent

▲ paper for recording data

Management

▲ Amount of time for the activity: 15–20 minutes

▲ Preparation time: none

▲ Group size: 1 large group (8 people or more)

Preparation and Setup

Activity Overview

A hand squeeze is propagated from person to person around a circle. The time it takes for the squeeze to go around the circle is measured, and the average response time per individual is calculated.

Concepts

❯ Sensory neurons conduct stimuli from a receptor to the spinal cord and on to the sensory cortex of the brain.

❯ Motor neurons conduct impulses from the motor cortex of the brain to muscles.

❯ Nerve impulses travel rapidly, but there is always a delay between stimulus and response.

Preparation

None.

Questions for Getting Started

❯ Tap your big toe with your finger. Trace the path of the nerve impulse you just created, from your toe to your brain.

❯ Do you have to think about a reflex, such as the movement of your knee when it's tapped? Can you trace the path of a reflex from the tap on the knee to the knee jerk?

After the Exploration

Expected Results

The response time per person is likely to be a bit shorter than 1 second, and it may be as fast as a third of a second. Generally, the response time will improve slightly with each subsequent trial of the activity. The most dramatic improvements occur between the first two or three trials, which is why it is important to have one or two practice runs before gathering data.

What's Going On?

The following sequence of events occurs in the nervous system of each person in the circle:

a. Pressure receptors in the left hand are triggered.

b. Nerve impulses generated by the pressure receptors travel along a sensory (afferent) nerve to the spinal cord.

c. The nerve impulses are conducted along tracts (bundles of nerve fibers) in the spinal cord up through the medulla, pons, and midbrain to the somatic sensory cortex of the brain.

d. The brain interprets the sensation as a "squeeze."

e. The primary motor cortex of the brain sends the instruction to use the right hand to squeeze the hand of the next person.

f. A nerve impulse travels from the primary motor cortex through the midbrain, pons, and medulla to the cortico-spinal tract within the spinal cord.

g. The impulse travels from the spinal cord to the hand along a motor (efferent) neuron.

h. The impulse reaches effectors (muscles in the hand and arm).

i. The muscles are instructed to squeeze the hand of the next person.

It is difficult to calculate exactly how long the process takes, because the speed with which nerve impulses travel varies from nerve to nerve. The larger the diameter of the nerve fiber, the more quickly an impulse travels. Impulses along nerves with myelin sheaths (those in the peripheral nervous system) travel much more quickly than unmyelinated nerves. Some large, myelinated nerves conduct nerve impulses at 200 meters per second, compared to only a few millimeters per second in small, unmyelinated nerve fibers. Another important variable is the response time of the brain itself, because it must use conscious thought to interpret the squeeze and make the decision to squeeze the other hand.

Discussion Questions

❶ When you sent the hand squeeze from the person on your left to the person on your right, was your nervous system using a reflex response? How was it the same as or different from a reflex?

❷ The average response time per person that you calculated is probably longer than the amount of time it actually takes. What are possible sources of error in the way you arrived at this average response time?

Going Further: Ideas for Inquiry

❯ Try the following variation to see if it reduces response time: Each person in the circle turns 90° to the right to face the back of the next person, and then places his or her dominant hand lightly on the shoulder of that next person. The activity is conducted the same as before, except that the "impulse" being propagated is a shoulder squeeze. Do the practice and three trials as before and calculate the average response time per person. Is this average response time different from the one you calculated for the hand squeeze? What do you think accounts for the difference?

❯ Try other ways of reducing the response time.

| The Basics and Beyond

Background

The nervous system has three major subunits: the central nervous system (CNS), the peripheral nervous system (PNS), and the autonomic nervous system (ANS). The central nervous system consists of the brain and spinal cord. The peripheral nervous system includes 12 pairs of cranial nerves that branch directly from the brain, 31 pairs of spinal nerves that branch from the spinal cord, and all the nerves that branch from these and form links between the CNS and all parts of the body. The ANS is largely separate from the other two systems and controls and coordinates the "automatic" basic life processes of the body, such as breathing, heartbeat, and digestion.

When a sensory nerve of the PNS receives a stimulus—such as a hand squeeze—a nerve impulse is relayed to the spinal cord and then to the brain. The brain interprets the stimulus and may send a message back to the PNS in response. For example, it may send an impulse through the spinal cord to motor nerves in the other hand, telling the muscles in that hand to squeeze. Nerve impulses make the round trip from the PNS to the CNS and back at lightning speed, but there is always a measurable delay between stimulus and response. This delay is called response time.

Tidbits

❭ The human body contains billions of nerves.

❭ An adult has about 75 kilometers (46 miles) of nerve fibers.

Explorer's Guide
Veins in Your Feet

Find out how blood in your veins can flow up to your heart

How does blood defy gravity and travel up your arms and legs? This experiment will show you how this happens.

Things You Will Need

▲ access to a watch or clock with a second hand

▲ paper for recording observations

To Do and Notice

You will need a partner to do this experiment. One of you will be the subject, while the other acts as the investigator. Then you will switch roles.

❶ Subject: Remove your shoes and socks. Stand perfectly still for 1 minute.

❷ Investigator: Note the appearance of the veins in the subject's feet.

❸ Subject: After a minute of standing still, take eight to ten quick steps in place.

❹ Investigator: Immediately look at the veins in the subject's feet again. Observe for about 1 minute. Record your observations.

❺ Switch roles.

Interpreting Your Observations

What happened to the veins in your feet when you stood still? After you stepped in place? What do these observations suggest about the movement of blood in the veins?

Facilitator's Guide

Veins in Your Feet

Materials

for each pair

▲ access to a clock or watch with a second hand

▲ paper for recording observations

Management

▲ Amount of time for the activity: 10–15 minutes

▲ Preparation time: none

▲ Group size: 2

Preparation and Setup

Activity Overview

Discover the role that muscular contraction plays in moving blood through the veins.

Concepts

❯ Veins are the blood vessels that conduct blood from tissues all over the body back to the heart.

❯ The pressure inside veins is typically very low as compared to the pressure inside arteries.

❯ One-way valves inside the veins of the arms and legs keep blood from flowing backwards.

❯ Muscular contractions of the arms and legs compress the veins and force blood through the one-way valves toward the heart.

Preparation

None.

Questions for Getting Started

❯ What is blood pressure? Have you ever had your blood pressure measured? What do the numbers mean?

❯ Can you trace the flow of blood through your body? How does this blood return to your heart? Why is blood pumped through the lungs?

TIP!

● You may want to warn explorers a day in advance that they will be removing their shoes and socks for this activity. Even with a warning, however, some may be shy about showing their bare feet. If this is the case, it may help to ask a few volunteers to do the activity and have others observe.

After the Exploration

Expected Results

The veins in the feet will swell as a subject remains still. After the subject steps in place for awhile, the veins appear collapsed, and then rapidly begin to swell again.

What's Going On?

While the subject remains still, blood accumulates in the veins of the feet. Without muscular contractions the blood cannot move toward the heart, and the veins swell. When the subject steps in place, his or her muscles compress the veins, forcing the accumulated blood through the one-way valves of the veins and eventually on to the heart. Because much of the blood they contained has been squeezed out of them by the muscular contractions, the veins appear collapsed immediately after the stepping movements. But blood begins to accumulate in the veins after the movement stops, and the veins again become swollen.

Discussion Questions

❶ Many people believe that inverted postures, such as headstands, are good for your heart and circulatory system. Can you figure out the logic behind this belief? Do you agree with it?

❷ Have you ever quickly gotten up from lying down or squatting and become dizzy? Can you relate this feeling to blood pressure?

Going Further: Ideas for Inquiry

❯ Can you think of an experiment that would help you tell the difference between arteries and veins in your arms? You can reproduce an experiment first done by William Harvey in the 1600s. Until Harvey did this experiment, people believed that blood shifted back and forth in blood vessels in a way similar to how tides move at sea.

❯ Find a volunteer with prominent blood vessels in his or her arms. Press your finger along one of the blood vessels. As you continue pressing, move the finger toward the upper arm. Notice what happens to the blood vessel behind the point of pressure. Next, press your finger along the blood vessel, but move your finger toward the lower arm. What happens to the vessel behind the pressure point now? Use your results and your knowledge of the direction of blood flow in veins to determine if it's a vein or an artery. Try the same experiment with different blood vessels.

The Basics and Beyond

Background

The blood vessels of the body are classified as either arteries or veins. Arteries carry blood away from the heart, and veins carry it back to the heart.

Arteries have thick walls to accommodate the high pressure of the flowing blood pumped by the heart. With the exception of the pulmonary artery—which carries deoxygenated blood to the lungs for re-oxygenation—the arteries carry oxygenated blood to the tissues of the body. Larger arteries branch into smaller arterioles, and then into tiny capillaries; this is where the oxygen in the blood diffuses into tissues and waste carbon dioxide from the tissues diffuses into the blood cells.

Blood then flows from the capillaries into venules, and then into veins, on its return journey to the heart. Blood pressure in the veins is much lower than in arteries; therefore, veins are thin-walled.

In the veins of the arms and legs, blood has to flow "uphill" much of the time on its way back to the heart. How is this gravity-defying feat accomplished? Movement of the arms and legs causes muscles to compress the veins. This compression squeezes the blood through the veins and forces open one-way valves that snap shut after the blood has passed through. These one-way valves prevent the backward flow of blood in the veins.

Tidbits

❯ There are about 96,000 kilometers (59,520 miles) of blood vessels (arteries, veins, and capillaries) in the body, enough to stretch almost 2.5 times around the equator!

❯ At any one time, about 75% of your blood is in your veins, 20% in your arteries, and 5% in your capillaries.

❯ People who stand for long periods of time at their jobs have increased venous pressure in their legs. This can cause veins to widen, making the one-way valves ineffective. Blood flowing backward can accumulate and lead to permanently swollen varicose veins.

Explorer's Guide

A Knight in Shining Newspaper

Estimate the surface area of your birthday suit

What is your body's largest organ? It's not your brain, your liver, or your lungs. It's your skin! Make a newspaper suit to help you estimate just how large this very important organ is.

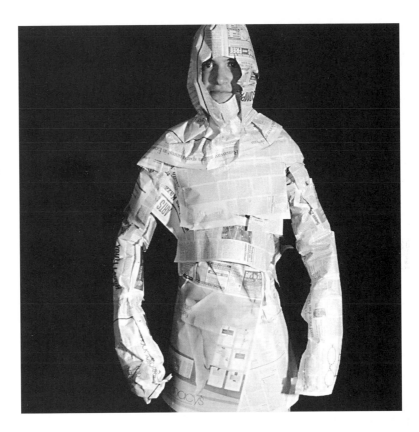

Things You Will Need

- ▲ about 10 large sheets of newspaper
- ▲ scissors
- ▲ tape
- ▲ meterstick or ruler
- ▲ open floor space

To Do and Notice

You'll need a partner or a few other explorers to do this activity.

There are two ways that this activity can be done. Read both "Method A" and "Method B," and choose the way you like best.

Method A

One person will be wrapped in newspaper, and a partner or other explorers will do the wrapping and measuring. You may wrap and measure the subject's entire body, or do one body part at a time.

❶ Decide who will be wrapped in newspaper.

❷ Begin wrapping newspaper snugly around each body part of the subject. Secure the pieces of newspaper with tape. It's okay if pieces of newspaper overlap.

❸ Don't worry about small areas of the body such as between fingers and toes. You may cover the entire hand or foot to save time. Don't forget the head and the bottoms of the feet.

❹ After a body part (or the entire body) is covered in paper, cut the paper off the subject's body. Be careful! Don't cut any clothing or skin! Try to keep all overlapped pieces of paper in their overlapped positions. Add more tape if you need to.

❺ When you are done, lay all the parts from the paper "suit" on the floor. Try to form a rectangle. You may cut some of the larger pieces of paper to form a rectangular shape.

❻ Measure the length and width of the rectangle. Multiply the length by the width to determine the area of the paper suit. This area is an estimate of the surface area of the subject's skin.

❼ Estimate the size of someone else's skin if you have time.

Caution:
Be careful not to cut any clothing or skin.

Method B

❶ Decide whose "birthday suit" will be measured.

❷ Have that person lie on sheets of newspaper. The partner or another team member should outline his or her form.

❸ To account for the thickness of the subject's body, measure the average width of the torso in the outline, and add half this width all around the outline.

❹ Cut out the modified outline, then cut the outline into pieces that will form a rectangle.

❺ Find the approximate surface area (width times height). Then multiply by 2 to account for both the front and back of the body.

❻ Estimate the size of someone else's skin if you have time.

Analyzing Data and Drawing Conclusions

Is the surface area of the subject's skin larger or smaller than you expected? Do you think your measurement underestimates or overestimates the true surface area? What else do you need to know about the size of the skin to compare it to the size of other organs in the body?

Facilitator's Guide
A Knight in Shining Newspaper

Materials

for each pair or small group

▲ about 10 large sheets of newspaper
▲ scissors
▲ tape
▲ meterstick or ruler
▲ open floor space

Management

▲ Amount of time for the activity:
30–45 minutes
▲ Preparation time: none
▲ Group size: 2–4 (same gender if possible)

TIPS!

● Collect surface-area estimates from all the small groups. The median value among them is likely to be the best collective estimate of the skin's surface area.

● Here's an alternative method for finding the area of the suit: Predetermine the area of 1 gram of newspaper. Have the explorers crumple the paper suits (being careful to remove overlapping seams), find the mass of the paper, then calculate the area of the paper.

Preparation and Setup

Activity Overview

Make a newspaper "suit" to estimate the surface area of the skin.

Concepts

❯ Skin is the largest organ of the human body.

❯ The skin serves many important body functions, including providing a protective barrier, regulating body temperature, and housing touch sensors.

❯ We continually shed and regenerate our skin.

Preparation

None, except for obtaining materials.

Questions for Getting Started

❯ What are the functions of the skin?

❯ Some animals, such as snakes, shed their skin in large sections. Do we shed our skin, too?

After the Exploration

Expected Results

The area of the newspaper suit is a rough approximation of the total surface area of the subject's skin. Estimates derived from this method will vary depending on the size of the person who is wrapped and the care taken in wrapping, cutting, and assembling the pieces. The surface area of an average adult male's skin is approximately 1.86 m^2 (20 ft^2) and that of an average adult woman is 1.58 m^2 (17 ft^2).

What's Going On?

The wrapping underestimates surface area because it doesn't take into account the finer detail of the body's surface (such as the area between the fingers), but error from the looseness of the wrapping and the laying out of the pieces compensates for some of this underestimation.

Discussion Questions

❶ What are some of the physical challenges faced by people with severe burns?

❷ What causes skin to wrinkle with age? What parts of the body do you think are most affected by wrinkling? Why?

Going Further: Ideas for Inquiry

❯ Calculate the volume of your skin using 2 mm as the average thickness and your estimate in this activity as the surface area. What would you need to know to calculate the mass of your skin?

The Basics and Beyond

Background

Skin, which covers the entire surface of the human body, is the body's largest organ. It carries out many life-sustaining functions, including protecting our inner organs from toxins, damage, and infection; providing a waterproof barrier; maintaining our internal fluids; regulating temperature (by sweating); eliminating wastes (also by sweating); synthesizing vitamin D; and sensing touch, pressure, temperature, and pain.

The skin has two basic layers: the epidermis and the dermis. The epidermis is made up largely of dead surface skin cells, the pigment melanin, and keratin, a protein that gives the skin surface a tough, waterproof coating. The dermis lies below the epidermis and contains hair follicles, blood vessels, nerves, sweat and oil glands, and muscle. All of these components are connected by the protein collagen.

Tidbits

❯ The average thickness of human skin is about 2 mm. The thinnest skin—only 0.5 mm thick—is on the eyelids. The 6-mm-thick skin on the soles of the feet is as thick as it gets.

❯ Household dust is made up mostly of dead skin cells. We lose millions of skin cells every day at an average of 50,000 skin cells per minute. In a year, we lose approximately 2 kg of skin and hair.

Appendix

How This Book Came to Be

Human Body Explorations was conceived and incubated within the Exploratorium's Teacher Institute, which offers programs designed especially for middle school and high school teachers. Teachers who participate in the Teacher Institute's programs work with exhibits and conduct explorations in a hands-on, inquiry-based manner. In the process, they expand their knowledge of scientific content, improve their pedagogical skills, and return to their classrooms armed with explorations and activities that they can use to engage the natural excitement and curiosity of their students.

Institute staff consistently heard a cry from biology and life sciences teachers for more useful classroom resources—and we decided to work with these teachers to create a life sciences resource that addressed their needs. We chose the human body as the topic because of its universal appeal to learners of all ages. This book is the result of our efforts.

Teachers were involved in every phase of the design and development of these explorations. More than a hundred classroom teachers from around the country tested the activities in their classrooms, providing us with invaluable feedback that helped us refine each of the explorations.

A Word About Inquiry

Science is a process of inquiry. The diverse ways in which scientists study the natural world and propose explanations derived from their work can all be described as aspects of inquiry. In recognition of the importance of inquiry in science—and in science education—the National Research Council, in its *National Science Education Standards*, specifies "science as inquiry" as a content standard for all grade levels.

Inquiry-based instruction can take many forms, but its basic principle is to parallel the scientific process. Elements of instructional inquiry include asking questions that can be answered through scientific investigations; designing and conducting scientific investigations; using a variety of tools and techniques, including mathematics and computers, to gather, analyze, and interpret data; developing explanations, predictions, and models using evidence; and thinking critically and logically to move from evidence to explanation.

Three general forms of instructional inquiry are *structured inquiry*, in which learners are provided with the problem, methods, and materials, but not the outcome; *guided inquiry*; in which only the problem and materials are given; and *open inquiry*, in which learners must develop their own questions and the means to answer them.

Most of the explorations in this book are written as structured inquiry. They provide the learner with a strong foundation by modeling the elements of scientific inquiry. As learners gain experience, they should be encouraged to move on to guided and open forms of inquiry, which involve asking their own questions, designing their own explorations, and satisfying their own curiosity. The suggestions in Going Further: Ideas for Inquiry, provided for each activity, are designed to get explorers moving in the direction of guided or open inquiry.

A thorough discussion of inquiry-based learning is provided in *Inquiry: Thoughts, Views, and Strategies for the K–5 Classroom* (1999), Volume 2 of the Foundations series published by the National Science Foundation. Although examples are from K–5 situations, the principles of inquiry are universal.

National Research Council Science Education Standards

In 1996, the National Research Council, a division of the National Academy of Sciences, published the *National Science Education Standards*. The goal of these standards is to provide guidance for curriculum development and formal teaching that will provide the best opportunity for all students to become scientifically literate. These standards emphasize a new way of teaching and learning about science that reflects how science itself is done, emphasizing inquiry as a way of achieving knowledge and understanding about the world. The *Standards* also address assessment of student performance, and teacher education and professional development. *Human Body Explorations* has been written with the *Standards* in mind. The standards that are addressed by the explorations in this book are listed below.

Copies of the *National Science Education Standards* (National Academy Press, Washington, D.C., 1996) are available from the National Academy Press (1-800-624-6242). The text of the *Standards* is available on the Internet at www.nas.edu.

All the investigations in *Human Body Explorations* satisfy Professional Development Standard A ("professional development for teachers of science requires learning essential science content through the perspectives and methods of inquiry"). In addition, the explorations satisfy these Content Standards:

Category	Grades 5–8 Standards	Grades 9–12 Standards
Science as Inquiry	• Abilities necessary to do science inquiry • Understandings about scientific inquiry	• Abilities necessary to do science inquiry • Understandings about scientific inquiry
History and Nature of Science	• Nature of science	• Nature of scientific knowledge

Other standards, and how they apply to each activity, are shown in the charts on the next two pages. You may be able to carry out any particular activity in such a way that it covers additional standards.

National Research Council Science Content Standards
Grades 5–8

ACTIVITY	Unifying Concepts and Processes			Life Science			Science in Personal and Social Perspectives
	Change, constancy, and measurement	Evidence, models, and explanation	Form and function	Structure and function in living systems	Reproduction and heredity	Regulation and behavior	Personal health
Naked Egg	✔	✔	✔	✔		✔	
Cellular Soap Opera		✔	✔	✔		✔	
Acid in Your Stomach	✔	✔		✔			✔
How Much Do You C?	✔	✔		✔			✔
How Sweet It Is	✔	✔		✔			
Milk Makes Me Sick!	✔	✔		✔	✔		✔
Got Blood?				✔			
Mother and Child Reunion		✔		✔	✔		
Fruitful DNA Extraction				✔			
What You Can't See *Can* Hurt You	✔	✔		✔		✔	✔
The Domino Effect				✔			
You've Got Your Nerve!	✔	✔	✔	✔			
The Arctic in a Cup	✔	✔		✔		✔	
Tunnel of Light	✔	✔	✔	✔		✔	
Something in Your Eye			✔	✔			
A "Hole" New Experience	✔		✔	✔			
The Taste of Color				✔		✔	
Are You a Supertaster?	✔	✔		✔	✔	✔	
The Nose Knows				✔		✔	
Nose-stalgia				✔			
Merry-Go-Round Illusion		✔		✔		✔	
Do You Know Where Your Hands Are?		✔		✔		✔	
aMAZE-ing Memories	✔					✔	
Riddle of the Sphincter	✔	✔		✔			
Sweaty Fingers		✔	✔	✔		✔	
Circle of Nerves	✔			✔		✔	
Veins in Your Feet		✔	✔	✔			
A Knight in Shining Newspaper	✔		✔	✔			

National Research Council Science Content Standards

Grades 9–12

ACTIVITY	Unifying Concepts and Processes			Life Science				Science in Personal and Social Perspectives
	Change, constancy, and measurement	Evidence, models, and explanation	Form and function	The cell	Matter, energy, and organization in living systems	Behavior of organisms	Molecular basis of heredity	Personal and community health
Naked Egg	✔	✔	✔	✔				
Cellular Soap Opera		✔	✔	✔	✔	✔		
Acid in Your Stomach	✔	✔		✔	✔			✔
How Much Do You C?	✔	✔		✔	✔			✔
How Sweet It Is	✔	✔		✔	✔			
Milk Makes Me Sick!	✔	✔		✔	✔			✔
Got Blood?				✔				
Mother and Child Reunion		✔		✔				
Fruitful DNA Extraction				✔			✔	
What You Can't See *Can* Hurt You	✔	✔		✔	✔		✔	✔
The Domino Effect				✔				
You've Got Your Nerve!	✔	✔	✔	✔	✔			
The Arctic in a Cup	✔	✔			✔			
Tunnel of Light	✔	✔	✔			✔		
Something in Your Eye		✔			✔			
A "Hole" New Experience	✔		✔					
The Taste of Color						✔		
Are You a Supertaster?	✔	✔		✔		✔		
The Nose Knows				✔		✔		
Nose-stalgia					✔			
Merry-Go-Round Illusion		✔				✔		
Do You Know Where Your Hands Are?		✔			✔	✔		
aMAZE-ing Memories	✔					✔		
Riddle of the Sphincter	✔	✔			✔			
Sweaty Fingers		✔	✔		✔	✔		
Circle of Nerves	✔				✔	✔		
Veins in Your Feet		✔	✔		✔			
A Knight in Shining Newspaper	✔		✔		✔			

Using Nonmetric Glassware and Measuring Devices

Many of our explorations include materials such as beakers, graduated cylinders, and flasks. If laboratory glassware is not available, common kitchen measuring cups and spoons, and glass or plastic cups can often be used instead. Similarly, if you have only a Fahrenheit thermometer or a scale reading in pounds, you can convert the temperatures and masses listed in the explorations into their English equivalents.

To help you successfully negotiate these substitutions, we've included below a simple metric conversion table and, for volume measurements, some suggestions for alternative measuring devices.

Volume

1 milliliter (mL) = 0.03 fluid ounces (fl oz)
30 mL = 1 fl oz
5 mL = 1 teaspoon (tsp)
15 mL = 1 tablespoon (Tbsp)
240 mL = 1 cup

Examples:
- A cup slightly larger than 16 oz can replace a 500 mL beaker
- Use a 3.5-oz or larger cup to substitute for a 100-mL beaker
- To measure 25 mL, use 1 tablespoon plus 2 teaspoons
- To measure 100 mL of a liquid, add together one-quarter cup (60 mL), 2 tablespoons (30 mL), and 2 teaspoons (10 mL)

Mass

1 gram (g) = 0.035 ounce (oz)
28 g = 1 oz

Temperature

To convert degrees Celsius (°C) to degrees Fahrenheit (°F):

Multiply °C by $\frac{9}{5}$, then add 32

To convert degrees Fahrenheit (°F) to degrees Celsius (°C):

Subtract 32 from °F and multiply by $\frac{5}{9}$

Topic Clusters

The explorations in this book are grouped into Part 1 or Part 2 depending on whether the aspect of the body they explore is hidden or easily seen. For readers who want to know which explorations relate to particular biological topics, we present the following list. The last topic cluster, *Mathematics as a Tool*, identifies explorations that involve the use of math skills.

Anatomy
Something in Your Eye
A "Hole" New Experience
Are You a Supertaster?
Riddle of the Sphincter
Sweaty Fingers
Veins in Your Feet
A Knight in Shining Newspaper

Biochemistry
Acid in Your Stomach
How Much Do You C?
How Sweet It Is
Milk Makes Me Sick!
Fruitful DNA Extraction

Cell Biology
Naked Egg
Cellular Soap Opera
The Domino Effect
You've Got Your Nerve!

Genetics
Milk Makes Me Sick!
Fruitful DNA Extraction
Got Blood?
Mother and Child Reunion

Health
Acid in Your Stomach
How Much Do You C?
Milk Makes Me Sick!
What You Can't See *Can* Hurt You

Neurosciences
The Domino Effect
You've Got Your Nerve!
Tunnel of Light
A "Hole" New Experience
Nose-stalgia
Do You Know Where Your Hands Are?
aMAZE-ing Memories
Circle of Nerves
Sweaty Fingers

Nutrition and Digestion
Acid in Your Stomach
How Much Do You C?
How Sweet It Is
Milk Makes Me Sick!
Riddle of the Sphincter

Physiology
Naked Egg
How Sweet It Is
Milk Makes Me Sick!
Domino Effect
You've Got Your Nerve!
Tunnel of Light
The Nose Knows
Merry-Go-Round Illusion
Riddle of the Sphincter
Sweaty Fingers
Veins in Your Feet

The Senses
Tunnel of Light
A "Hole" New Experience
Something in Your Eye
The Taste of Color
Are You a Supertaster?
The Nose Knows
Nose-stalgia
Merry-Go-Round Illusion
The Arctic in a Cup

Mathematics as a Tool
Naked Egg
Acid in Your Stomach
How Much Do You C?
You've Got Your Nerve!
A "Hole" New Experience
Riddle of the Sphincter
Circle of Nerves
A Knight in Shining Newspaper

Resource Guide

Textbooks

Many textbooks in general biology and anatomy and physiology are available to use for general reference. We recommend the following two because they are clear, complete, and have an abundance of illuminating illustrations:

Biology (5th edition), Neil A. Campbell, Jane B. Reece, and Lawrence G. Mitchell, Addison Wesley, 1999

Essentials of Human Anatomy and Physiology (4th edition), Elaine Marieb, Addison Wesley, 1996

"Coloring Books"

Complex anatomical and physiological details are well-illustrated and easy to understand in the coloring-book type of publication. The following are useful for those interested in learning more about the human body:

Anatomy Coloring Book (2nd edition), Wynn Kapit and Lawrence M. Elson, Addison Wesley, 1993

The Biology Coloring Book, Robert D. Griffin, Harper and Row, 1986

The Human Brain Coloring Book, Marian C. Diamond, Arnold B. Scheibel, and Lawrence M. Elson, HarperCollins, 1985

The Physiology Coloring Book, Wynn Kapit, Robert I. Macey, and Esmail Meisami, Addison Wesley Longman, 1987

General Audiences

The following books for the general public are excellent sources of information about the workings of the brain, the nervous system, and the senses:

The Human Mind Explained, Susan A. Greenfield, ed., Henry Holt, 1996

A Natural History of the Senses, Diane Ackerman, Vintage Press, 1990

Sources of Materials

The vast majority of the materials used in these explorations are easily obtained from grocery stores and pharmacies. You may be able to save substantially by purchasing large quantities of materials, if they are available, at discount warehouse outlets.

Carolina Biologicals (1-800-334-5551) is an excellent source of classroom laboratory supplies and chemicals. The listings under "Laboratory Equipment and Supplies" in your local Yellow Pages may help you to locate local sources for laboratory-specific materials.

An excellent source of chemicals at very good prices is Sigma Chemicals (1-800-368-4661).

Acknowledgments

At the Exploratorium, no one works alone. *Human Body Explorations* would not have been possible without the creativity, critical feedback, and support of the staff of the Teacher Institute and other museum staff members, along with many teachers and scientists from outside the museum. To all these people, who are listed below, we offer our sincere thanks. In addition, we want to thank Goéry Delacôte, Rob Semper, and Dennis Bartels for providing the institutional backing necessary to transform this project from a vision into a reality.

Preston Addison
Nick Alesandro
Jhina Alvarado
Annette Anzalone
Luis Araquistain
Lauralee Barton
Linda Bartoshuk
Robert Beauchamp
Allsion Belt
Julie Berger
Marc Borbely
Ruth Brown
Charles Carlson
Judy Chang
Edmund Chu
Cesar Dayco
Nancy Defensor
Dan DeFoe
Paul Doherty
Laura Edenborough-Lewis
Melanie Encinas
Pam Ferris
Tom Finger
Ken Finn
Mary Fish
Robin Franklin
Maren Friesen
Debbie Geary
Karen Goldman
Marian Gonzalez
Linda Gostinger
Kim Hansen Guzman
Theresa Heckathorne
John Holley
K. E. Hones
Judy Hsu
Jennifer Huntsberger

Michele Ignoffo
Barb Jacobsen
Katherine A. Jezidija
Debbie Jones
Andrea Kean
Burt Kessler
Eric Kielich
James Kliewer
JoAnn Knecht
Jennifer Koren-Levine
Lori Lambertson
Sue Lee
Arlette Manders
Rosanna Mariotti
Joanne McLean
Karen Mendelow
Arthur Morrill
Dean Muller
Eric Muller
Joan Murphy
Nancy Newman
Linda Ng
Thomas O'Bier
Heather O'Connor
Travis Parker
David S. Peek
Sandra Petersen
Gail Purtell
Sarah Rezny
Sandra Robins
Sam Roemer
Lisa Sardinia
Debbie Schmalz
Mike Schulist
Betsy Schulz
Douglas Scott
Patricia Sempell
Susan Sherman
Linda Shore

Sheila Smith
Kristen Sorensen
Mary Stemmler
Sylvia Stevens
Sean Stoops
Elena Stowell
Dacotah Swett
Rob Swezey
Modesto Tamez
Zachary Tobias
Beth Touchette-Laughlin
Ronna Voorsanger
Gwendolyn Watson
Kim Wegesin
Dana Wickner
Suzanne Wiersema-Menard
David Woulfin
Julie Yu

Glossary

acidic: Refers to a solution in which hydrogen ions predominate.

acid: Compound that can add hydrogen ions to a solution, lowering the *pH.*

action potential: A change in electrical potential across a neuron's cell membrane during transmission of a *nerve impulse.*

adipose tissue: Body tissue made of cells that contain large amounts of fat, used to store energy and insulate and protect organisms.

adrenal gland: Glands located above the kidneys that release the *hormones adrenaline* and *noradrenaline* in response to a threat, producing bodily changes such as increase in heart rate, blood pressure, and blood glucose levels.

alkaline: Refers to a solution in which hydroxide ions predominate, giving it a basic *pH.*

alkaloid: Any of a diverse group of plant-derived compounds that typically have powerful physiological effects on humans. Alkaloids can be recognized by their bitter taste.

allele: Alternative forms of the same gene. For example, the alleles for blue and brown eye color are variants of the eye color *gene.*

amino acid: A class of compounds that can link together to form *proteins.*

anion: An atom or group of atoms that has lost one or more electrons, making it negatively charged.

antibody: Protective molecule produced by an organism in response to invading microbes or other foreign particles. Antibodies render these "invaders" harmless by binding to them.

antigen: A molecule on the surface of a cell, substance, or microbe that the body recognizes as "self" or a "nonself" invader.

antioxidant: A compound that slows the rate at which substances react with oxygen. Reaction with oxygen can damage cells and cellular components.

antiserum: Blood serum containing molecules (known as *antibodies*) that can fight infection. Animals produce antiserums in response to invading microbes or other foreign particles.

arteria centralis retinae: The *artery* that delivers oxygen and nutrients to the light-sensitive cells at the back of the eye.

arteriole: Small blood vessel that carries blood from *arteries* to *capillaries,* on its way from the heart to the body's tissues.

artery: Blood vessel that carries blood away from the heart.

auditory: Relating to the ear or sense of hearing.

auditory nerve: Nerve that sends sensory signals from the ear to the brain.

autonomic nervous system: The part of the nervous system in vertebrate animals that controls involuntary processes such as heart rate and gland secretions.

axon: Long section of a nerve cell that relays impulses away from the cell body and toward other nerves, organs, or the brain.

base: Compound that can reduce the concentration of hydrogen ions in a solution, raising the *pH.*

blind spot: The point of attachment where blood vessels and the *optic nerve* enter and exit the back of the eye. No image can be created here because there are no light-sensitive cells in this area. Also known as *optic disk.*

blood type/blood group: Classification of human blood determined by the presence or absence of specific compounds (known as *antigens*) on the surface of red blood cells.

bronchiole: Small air tube in the lungs that end in air sacs known as alveoli.

capillary: Tiny blood vessel through which oxygen and nutrients in the blood diffuse into tissues, and carbon dioxide and other wastes from the tissue diffuse into blood cells.

carbohydrate: Any of a large class of compounds, consisting of sugars and starches, that provide energy and energy-storage materials for living organisms.

carbonyl: A carbon atom double-bonded to an oxygen atom. This chemical group is typically available to participate in chemical reactions.

cellular respiration: A series of chemical reactions in cells that breaks down substances to produce energy. Respiration requires oxygen.

central nervous system: Structures (in vertebrates, the brain and spinal cord) that coordinate activities of the entire nervous system.

cerebral cortex: Largest and most complex part of mammalian brain containing sensory and motor *neurons;* part of vertebrate brain most changed through evolution.

chemosense: A sense (such as smell) that involves the detection of gaseous or volatile molecules.

chromosome: Structure inside the cell nucleus composed of *DNA* and *protein.*

codominant: Refers to two equally dominant *alleles* that control the same characteristic, give different instructions, and are expressed in the organism. One example is the human blood group AB, in which both the A and B alleles are expressed.

collagen: A *protein* present in connective tissue of skin, tendons, and bone.

conduction: The passage of heat from hotter bodies to cooler bodies. Conduction occurs when more energetic (hotter) molecules collide with their less energetic (cooler) neighbors and pass on some of their energy.

cone: Light receptor at the back of the eye that converts visual information into nerve impulses sent to the brain. Cones are specialized to detect color.

cornea: A layer of transparent tissue at the front of the eye that helps the lens focus images on the *retina*.

denature: To unfold the three-dimensional structure of a *protein*.

dendrite: Branching structure found on the cell body of a nerve cell that receives nerve impulses and conveys them toward the cell body.

depolarization: A decrease in electrical potential difference across a nerve's cell membrane when the nerve is transmitting an impulse.

dermis: In vertebrates, the innermost and thicker skin layer. The dermis lies below an outer skin layer (the *epidermis*) and contains hair follicles, blood vessels, nerves, sweat and oil glands, and muscle.

diffusion: Movement of particles from an area of high concentration to an area of low concentration.

disaccharide: Sugar molecule derived by the combination of two simple sugar molecules, or *monosaccharides*.

DNA: The genetic material found in living things.

dominant: An inheritance pattern in which the expression of a *gene* masks the expression of a different gene for the same trait. Because the *allele* for brown eyes is dominant over the allele for blue eyes, for instance, a person who has one allele for both brown and blue will have brown eye color.

double helix: The spiral ladder shape of *DNA* molecules.

eccrine sweat gland: Small gland in the skin that secretes sweat when the external temperature or body temperature is high, or in response to a variety of stimuli including pain, fear, and stress.

effector: A cell or organ that has a physiological response to a nerve impulse.

electromagnetic spectrum: Visible light and other forms of electromagnetic energy that radiate through space as waves of various lengths.

electron: Negatively charged, elementary particle found in all atoms.

endolymph: Fluid in the *semicircular canals* (in the inner ear) that moves in response to head and body movements, triggering nerve impulses to the brain.

enzyme: A substance in the body that speeds up chemical reactions.

epidermis: In vertebrates, the outer layer of skin made mostly of dead skin cells, the pigment *melanin,* and the protein *keratin*.

epiglottis: Flap of cartilage near the base of the tongue that helps prevent water and food from being inhaled into the lungs during swallowing.

epinephrine (adrenaline) **and norepinephrine** (noradrenaline)**:** *Hormones* that quickly prepare the body for a "fight or flight" response by increasing heart and breathing rate, blood glucose levels, and muscle power, and dilating the blood vessels in skeletal muscle.

esophagus: A muscular tube that propels food to the stomach by wavelike cycles of contractions.

fungiform papillae: Bumps covering the front two-thirds of the tongue that house the taste-detector organs known as *taste buds*.

gastroesophageal sphincter: A ring of muscle at the top of the stomach that allows food to enter, but not easily exit.

gene: A unit of coded instructions that controls the expression of an individual characteristic in an organism. Genes are located on an organism's *chromosomes*.

genotype: An organism's genetic makeup.

heat: Energy that flows from a body of higher temperature to a body of lower temperature.

hippocampus: A part of the vertebrate brain involved in formation and long-term storage of memories.

homeostasis: The regulation by a living organism of a stable inner environment.

hormone: "Messenger" compounds produced in one part of an organism that help regulate a range of activities in other areas of the body, such as growth and reproduction.

human genome: The complete set of *genes* in one human cell.

hydrophilic: Refers to substances that attract water.

hydrophobic: Refers to substances that repel water.

hydroxyl group: A chemical group consisting of one oxygen atom and one hydrogen atom.

hypothalamus: A part of the brain that controls many functions, such as body temperature, sleeping, and sexual behavior.

hypothermia: Abnormally low body temperature in warm-blooded organisms.

immune system: Special defense cells that protect against infection by attacking foreign particles and substances, such as viruses, bacteria, parasites, or transplanted organs.

invertase: A compound found in yeast that breaks down cane sugar (sucrose) into its component simple sugars, glucose and fructose.

involuntary muscle: Muscle that cannot be controlled by will.

ion: An atom or molecule that has lost or gained electrons, and therefore has an electrical charge.

iridescence: Rainbowlike colors visible in objects (like soap bubbles and some minerals) caused by interference of light.

iris: A muscular ring in the eye that changes its diameter to control the size of a central hole (called the *pupil*) and ensure that light enters the eye at an optimum level.

keratin: Any of a group of strong, elastic *proteins* found in hair, skin, feathers, hooves, and horns.

kinetic energy: The energy of an object due to its motion.

lactase: A substance in the body that breaks down a milk sugar known as *lactose* into the smaller molecules glucose and galactose.

lactose: The predominant sugar found in milk.

lactose intolerance: A disorder characterized by intestinal cramps and diarrhea caused by the body's inability to break down the milk sugar *lactose*.

larynx: Structure at the front of the windpipe that contains the vocal cords. Commonly known as the Adam's apple.

lens: The part of the eye that helps to focus images on the *retina*.

limbic system: A group of brain structures believed to be important in memory and the expression of emotions and instinctive behaviors.

macromolecule: Very large molecule.

melanin: Pigments found in the eye, hair, and skin of vertebrates. Melanin in the skin absorbs ultraviolet radiation, protecting cells from its damaging effects.

membrane potential: The difference in charge across a neuron's *plasma membrane*.

mole: A standard unit used to measure quantities of chemical substances.

monosaccharide: A simple sugar molecule, such as glucose.

motor neuron: Nerve that relays signals from the *central nervous system* to cells or organs, causing responses such as muscle contraction and secretion of substances from glands.

multiple sclerosis: A disorder of the nervous system in which the coverings of nerves (known as *myelin*) are broken down, resulting in interruption of *nerve impulses*.

myelin: A material that coats and insulates the axons of neurons in the *peripheral nervous system*, and enables fast transmission of impulses.

nerve impulse: Electrical signal that travels along nerves and help transmit information through the nervous system.

neuron: Nerve cell.

neurotransmitter: Chemical released by a *neuron* into the gap between nerve cells that helps transmit impulses to another neuron.

nontaster: Person who has a low density of *fungiform papillae* on his or her tongue, and may weakly perceive bitter tastes.

norepinephrine: See *epinephrine*.

nucleotide: Large molecule that links together in long chains that form *macromolecules* such as *DNA*.

nucleus: Membrane-bound structure inside all plant and animal cells containing the genetic material *DNA* and serving as the control center for cellular activities.

olfactory bulb: A part of the brain that connects with receptors in the nose responsible for perceiving smells.

olfactory receptor: Cell in the nasal passages that recognize different kinds of smells and sends smell information to the brain.

olfactory/olfaction: Relating to the sense of smell.

optic disk: See *blind spot*.

optic nerve: Nerve that carries visual information from the eye to the brain.

osmosis: Movement of water across a selectively permeable membrane from an area of high water concentration to an area of low water concentration.

papillae: Bumps on the surface of some organisms and organs, such as the tongue.

peripheral nervous system: Sensory and *motor neurons* that connect to the *central nervous system*.

peristalsis: Involuntary muscular contractions in the digestive tract that propel food along.

pH: A measure of the *acidity* or *alkalinity* of a solution, based on its concentration of hydrogen ions.

pharynx: Cavity connecting the mouth and esophagus through which food and respiratory gases pass.

phospholipids: Large molecules that are major components of cell membranes.

photopupillary reflex: Constriction of the pupil caused by light entering the eye.

photoreceptor: Cell that responds to light, usually by sending a *nerve impulse*. *Rods* and *cones* are photoreceptors found in the eyes of vertebrates.

plasma membrane: The semipermeable boundary on the surface of cells.

polar molecule: Molecule attracted to water because it has an uneven distribution of *electrons*.

polymer: A large, chainlike molecule made by linking many simple molecules.

potential energy: The energy stored in an object, such as a coiled spring, due to its position or shape. Electrical energy is one kind of potential energy.

precipitate: To come out of a liquid solution as a solid.

proprioceptor: Tiny sensor in muscles, tendons, joints, and ligaments that detects tension, elongation, and other changes, and helps judge body positions and maintain balance and posture.

protein: A large class of complex compounds essential for structure and chemical processes in all living organisms.

pulmonary artery: Blood vessel that carries deoxygenated blood from the right side of the heart to pick up oxygen in the lungs.

pupil: The opening through which light enters the eye.

reflex: An automatic response to a stimulus.

refractory period: The short period after a nerve cell has fired during which it cannot fire again.

repolarization: The diffusion of potassium ions from the inside to the outside of a *neuron* that restores the nerve cell's resting potential—the difference in electrical potential inside and outside a nerve that is not firing. Repolarization occurs after an impulse passes through the neuron.

resting membrane potential: The difference in electrical potential across a neuron's cell membrane when the *neuron* is not sending an impulse.

retina: The layer of light-sensitive cells at the back of the eye that receives visual information and transmits it to the brain for interpretation.

rhesus factor: Any of a group of compounds sometimes found on the surface of red blood cells, and used to classify human blood. Commonly called Rh factor.

rod: Light receptor at the back of the eye that converts visual information into nerve impulses that are sent to the brain. Rods sense black and white and help with night vision.

saccharidase: Compound that helps break down sugars.

semicircular canal: Sense organ in the inner ear that detects head movements.

sensory (afferent) neuron: Nerve that relays information about the external and internal environment to the spinal cord and brain.

serum: Liquid portion of the blood lacking the substances that form clots.

spinal cord: The part of the vertebrate *central nervous system* housed in the backbone.

sternum: Rod-shaped bone that attaches to the collarbone and most of the ribs. Also known as the breastbone.

supertaster: Person who has a high density of *fungiform papillae* on his or her tongue, and who may be especially sensitive to bitter tastes.

surface tension: Property of a liquid that allows its surface to act like an elastic substance. Some insects can stand on water, for example, because of the water's strong surface tension.

sympathetic nervous system: Part of the *(autonomic) nervous system* important in regulation of a range of processes, including sweat production, heart rate, blood vessel constriction, and salivary gland secretion.

synapse: The gap between adjacent *neurons* across which nerve impulses are transmitted.

tactile: Relating to the sense of touch.

taste bud: Small organ that contains taste receptor cells, found on the tongue in terrestrial animals.

taster: Person who has a moderate density of taste buds on his or her tongue, and who may perceive bitterness in foods, but not intensely so.

thalamus: Brain structure that plays a role in translating nerve impulses into sensations, and sends sensory information to the *cerebral cortex*.

thermal conductivity: A measure of how fast heat is transmitted in a substance.

trachea: Tube through which air passes from the throat to the lungs.

ultraviolet (UV) light: Electromagnetic radiation, invisible to the naked eye, with wavelengths shorter than violet light and longer than X rays.

vein: Blood vessel that carries blood toward the heart.

venule: Small blood vessel that transports deoxygenated blood from *capillaries* to *veins,* on its way to the heart.

vestibular system of the inner ear: A group of structures in the inner ear that helps vertebrates sense movement and maintain balance. The *semicircular canals* are part of this system.

vitamin: Compound present in foods that is essential for body growth and maintenance and regulation of metabolism.

vitamin C: A water-soluble *vitamin* found in fruits and vegetables.

wavelength: The distance from a point on a wave to the corresponding point on the adjacent wave.

About the Exploratorium

The Exploratorium is a hands-on museum of science, art, and human perception dedicated to discovery. Founded in San Francisco in 1969 by the noted physicist and educator Frank Oppenheimer, over the years it has grown into an internationally acclaimed science center. Its hundreds of interactive exhibits stimulate learning and richly illustrate scientific concepts and natural phenomena.

Since 1984, the Exploratorium's Teacher Institute has provided workshops for in-service science and math teachers of grades 6–12. The Institute offers a teacher-centered, learn-by-doing approach to science learning. Museum exhibits and classroom activities are used to explore science concepts and model inquiry-based pedagogy. Each summer, the Teacher Institute offers several institutes—intensive four-week, 100-hour programs—on a variety of science and math topics. Upon completion of the summer institutes, teachers become part of the Teacher Institute "family" of over 2000 alumni and are eligible to return for Saturday, after-school, and summer alumni workshops as well as other special programs.

You can visit us online at www.exploratorium.edu for more valuable science learning resources.

About the Author

Biologist Karen Kalumuck has been with the Exploratorium Teacher Institute since 1994 and has developed an exciting hands-on, inquiry-based teacher enhancement program for middle school and high school life sciences and biology teachers. Many of the activities in this book had their beginnings in Karen's Exploratorium classroom, where they were enthusiastically received by the participating teachers.

Before joining the Exploratorium, Karen earned a Ph.D. from Rice University for her work in genetics, after which she conducted research in the molecular biology of human genetic disease at Baylor College of Medicine. As a college professor, she taught a wide range of courses including cell biology, genetics, developmental biology, and anatomy and physiology.

Karen lives on the Pacific coast just south of San Francisco with her husband Rob Swezey. They share their home with three cats, two guinea pigs, a Vietnamese pot-bellied pig, and their dog Mollie.

Photo Credits

All photos © Exploratorium unless otherwise noted. Amy Snyder and Lily Rodriguez, staff photographers. Photo illustrations, David Barker. Pages 1, 3, 5, 6, 93: Debbie Geary; Pages 4, 9: Ronna Voorsanger; Pages 11, 24, 32, 38, 56, 83, 88, 120, 149: Karen Kalumuck; Page 29: © Peter Fox; Pages 44, 105, 110: Eric Kielich; Page 49: Will Mosgrove; Page 55: CORBIS/Richard T. Nowitz; Page 61: William Neill Photography; Page 81: CORBIS; Page 87: Paul Doherty; Page 113: CORBIS/Bettmann; Pages 147, 159: Uniphoto Stock Photography.